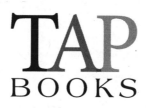

The Stone Thrower

The Stone Thrower

A Daughter's Lessons, A Father's Life

JAEL EALEY RICHARDSON

THOMAS ALLEN PUBLISHERS
TORONTO

Library and Archives Canada Cataloguing in Publication

Richardson, Jael Ealey, 1980–
The stone thrower : a daughter's lessons, a father's life / Jael Ealey Richardson.

Includes bibliographical references.
Issued also in electronic formats.
ISBN 978-1-77102-205-7

1. Ealey, Chuck. 2. Football players—Canada—Biography. 3. Canadian Football League—Biography. 4. Black Canadians—Biography. 5. Richardson, Jael Ealey, 1980– —Family. 6. Fathers and daughters—Canada—Biography. 7. Black Canadians—Race identity. I. Title.

GV939.E24R53 2012   796.335092   C2012-904613-2

For reasons of privacy, the names of some individuals have been changed.

Editor: Janice Zawerbny
Cover design: Karen Satok
Cover image: Courtesy of author

Published by Thomas Allen Publishers,
a division of Thomas Allen & Son Limited,
390 Steelcase Road East,
Markham, Ontario L3R 1G2 Canada

www.thomasallen.ca

We acknowledge the support of the Canada Council for the Arts, which last year invested $153 million to bring the arts to Canadians throughout the country, and the Ontario Arts Council for our publishing program. We also acknowledge the financial support of the Government of Ontario, through the Ontario Book Publishing Tax Credit and the Ontario Media Development Corporation, and the Government of Canada.

Nous remercions le Conseil des arts du Canada de son soutien. L'an dernier, le Conseil a investi 153 millions de dollars pour mettre de l'art dans la vie des Canadiennes et des Canadiens de tout le pays.

12 13 14 15 16 17 18   5 4 3 2

Printed and bound in Canada.

For my father

Being a Negro in America is not a comfortable existence. It means being a part of the company of the bruised, the battered, the scarred, and the defeated. Being a Negro in America means trying to smile when you want to cry. It means trying to hold on to physical life amid psychological death. It means the pain of watching your children grow up with clouds of inferiority in their mental skies. It means having your legs cut off, and then being condemned for being a cripple. It means seeing your mother and father spiritually murdered by the slings and arrows of daily exploitation, and then being hated for being an orphan . . . It means being harried by day and haunted by night by a nagging sense of nobodiness and constantly fighting to be saved from the poison of bitterness. It means the ache and anguish of living in so many situations where hopes unborn have died.

— MARTIN LUTHER KING JR.

Bringing the gifts that my ancestors gave,
I am the dream and the hope of the slave. I rise I rise I rise.

— MAYA ANGELOU

FOR MOST of my life I have felt watery like an ocean, my sense of self disoriented and bottomless, my blackness lost and out of place in a country known for cold winters, covered in whiteness. And I don't know how I got here, to this place of uncertainty. I just know it has something to do with my father.

Every time people ask me, where are you from, I give the same answer: "I was born here. I'm Canadian. My parents are American."

"But where are they *really* from?" they ask me.

I was never sure how to answer that, up until recently. I wasn't sure how to explain my history. I knew about slavery and the Underground Railroad. I knew that Harriet Tubman was the Moses of our people, that she brought thousands of slaves to safety on a metaphorical railroad where the final stop was the Promised Land of Canada. I knew about Martin Luther King Jr. and his faith-dream speech on the steps of the Lincoln Memorial. What was missing, however, was a clear understanding of my family history—the factors that influenced the life I know in Canada, starting with my father's arrival here in the seventies.

Everything I knew about my father's story was made up of what I had read in old newspaper articles in my parents' basement, and what I had heard about him on television. It was based on assumptions I made from my father's interviews about his time in professional football. My father and I had never spoken about what went on behind the well-known events of his story. He didn't like to talk about it. When asked direct questions, he was unapologetically elusive.

I didn't know where my grandmother was born or how she got to Portsmouth—the town where my father was raised. I didn't know anything about his life in the projects. I had never been to his hometown for a visit.

I wanted to know what happened to my grandfather. I wanted to know about my father's friends, his struggles as an adolescent. I wanted to know about the boy I had never met in the picture on my grandmother's side table. I wanted to understand why my father came to Canada, and why he chose to stay here. I wanted to understand why I have never felt black enough.

In America, where my mother and father were both born, blackness is measured in blood—the tiniest drop determining your connection to a history of disadvantages. In Canada, blackness is measured, not in blood, but in appearances and associations. People often say to me: You're not *really* black; because my mother looks white; because I have curly hair and fair skin; because I'm not from a country directly connected to the Caribbean or Africa; because I am friends with too many white people. In the summer of 2008, when I found out I was expecting my first child, I *needed* answers and resolution.

When an invitation arrived that same summer, inviting my father to his high school reunion during the town's homecoming weekend, I finally got my opportunity. My father asked me if I wanted to go down to Portsmouth with him. I tried to be like him when I responded—calm and collected. Even though inside I was flooded with excitement.

In Portsmouth, my father would open up for the first time about his childhood, and as he did, I would replace assumptions I had made about him as a child with observations formed from deeper, richer insights. I would learn things I never knew about my family through the stories of people who knew my father before I did.

In the months that followed the trip to Portsmouth, I would also discover things about American history and the civil rights movement that would deepen my understanding of black history. I would begin to resolve my doubts about whether or not I was black enough and what it meant to be Canadian—reflections that would influence my new life as a mother.

We bumped over a set of train tracks in Portsmouth, Ohio, in August 2008, when the air was sticky-thick like molasses. My mother was quiet; my brother and his son peered out the window in silence as my father drove across the tracks and into his old neighbourhood—his eyes focused on the road ahead of him. But I looked up and watched those train tracks disappear in the rear-view mirror for as long as they let me. I imagined the distant rumble and a rush of wind from a story I heard my father tell reporters when I was younger.

A boy of about ten, lean with a deep brown face that's serious and eyes that seem older, shuffle-drags his rubber-toed shoes past sleeping houses. Smeared, grey clouds dull the early glow of sunshine. He zips his coat and buries his hands in the pockets of his jeans. He heads down the road, towards the train tracks, as a breeze sweeps through leaves that rustle down the pavement beside him.

The tracks are dotted in shades of earth and grey—the in-betweens filled with small stones that are smooth and shapeless. The boy picks up a stone, his long fingers shifting it in the palm of his hand. He looks around the crossing, rolls the stone between his fingers. A faint, familiar whistle, a low, breathy ch-ch-ch-cha, ch-ch-ch-cha, sounds in the distance. A smile stretches slowly across his face. The train whistles louder as it curls around the corner. Full, black clouds rise in dense, dark puffs that swell in smoky rhythm. CH-ch-ch-ch-CHA, CH-ch-ch-ch-CHA. The train presses forward, boxcars piled with coal dragging behind the engine—each car stamped NORFOLK & WESTERN in faded yellow. The boy watches the train approach, expectant. He grabs a few stones, and squeezes them between his fingers. He waits a few yards back from the trembling railroad. The train moves faster and the ground rumbles as the train roars towards him. He selects a stone and pulls his arm back as a gust of wind rushes through him, the train passing quickly. He watches for the light between the cars, then throws, stone sailing. Ping. The rock hits the top of the train and sails in another direction. *Too high.* He selects a few more and waits. *Light. Throw.* The stone strikes the base of the speeding train with a loud thud. He narrows his eyes to focus. *Wait. Light. Throw.* The stone flies towards the coal train, the cars rocking with the rapid motion of the rails. BANG! The rock lands on the *N* and the boy shakes his fist in triumph. He draws out another stone. *Wait. Light. Throw.* BANG!

The boy visits the train tracks often after that day. He selects the stones, waits for the train, rush of wind, the streak of light, the *N* that follows. He learns to focus, to tune out the noise, so that his timing and aim are perfect. He learns to anticipate the moving cars so he always hits his target.

Forty years after my father left the segregated projects where a handful of stones and the Norfolk & Western coal train would transform my history, I pressed my forehead against the car window and let those train tracks roll into my memory. This is where it all began, I thought, as I smelled and stared and recited it. Like David and his sling of stones. This was the beginning of my story.

PORTSMOUTH
1950–1968

There is in this world no such force
as the force of a person determined to rise.
The human soul cannot be permanently chained.

W. E. B. DUBOIS

1

I AM THE DAUGHTER of someone famous, which most people think is ideal, thrilling. It certainly has its benefits. I can eat for free at a Lebanese restaurant and stay in a high-end hotel for next to nothing whenever I visit Toledo, the city where my father secured his stardom. The downside to being the daughter of someone famous is that up until a few years ago there were a ton of people who knew more about him than I did.

If someone asked me what I knew about my father when I was a teenager, there were four things I could have said about him, with a modest level of certainty, based on what I saw, what he told me, and where we went and didn't go when I was younger.

One. He was born in a place called Portsmouth. I didn't know what it looked like, because I had never been there, but I gathered from what he said, on the few occasions it was mentioned, that it was small. I also gathered that when he lived there he was poor, because in the winter when it snowed heavy and my siblings and I asked for a ride to school, he told us that *he* used to walk up a hill barefoot to get to school—when snow was nearly at his waist. I knew there was a place called the North End, and I imagined it was full of poor black people. I imagined it looked like the black neighbourhoods I saw on TV and in the movies I went to at the local Cineplex Odeon—black people on rickety porches playing dominoes, talking about the way things used to be as they swayed back and forth on rocking chairs. I imagined it smelled like smoky pipes and iced tea.

Two. He played football at the University of Toledo. That was where his fame began. Whenever we visited Toledo, everyone recognized him; they wanted to shake his hand, and get his autograph. I knew his number was retired, because it was on display at the university, and because he got it unretired for my brother who also went to school there around the time a large mural of my father was painted a few stories high on the side of the stadium. It's pretty cool to see your name on display like that. It's why I will never change my last name, even if I get married. Toledo feels different, and I don't like to go there that often because there's nothing much to do, but there my family is famous. In Toledo, being an Ealey makes you a celebrity.

Three. He played in the CFL for a few years. Won a Grey Cup, and wore an orange coat as a commentator for the CBC, although I didn't witness any of this. I gathered all of this from pictures in the basement, along with the display of trophies that were covered in dust, because my mother said it was a pain to clean them. I could see why. There were a lot of them. There were so many trophies, and I had no idea what they were for. It was hard to read them, even on the shelves where they were lined up like soldiers. I was afraid I would knock them over. I was afraid I would break the arm off the man with the football in his hands, which reminded me of a wedding couple cake topper. Only the guys on the cakes were happy, just-got-married, white guys, and the guys on my dad's trophies looked serious and weathered; they were a tarnished shade of black-brown.

Four. He worked in investment. I didn't know much about this, but I gathered that he must like his job, because he spent a lot of time there and never complained, except about the drive.

His office was on the other side of the city and it took him over an hour to get there.

I often wished he was home more—although I never said that to him. I wished I knew more about him. I never told him that either.

I had a clear sense of what I wanted to learn about my father and my history when I went to Portsmouth for the first time. I wanted to know what his life looked like before the fame and the privilege. I wanted to understand how hard it was to live in and get out of the projects.

The things that I learned in Portsmouth, however, prompted even more questions about my father's life, questions that forced me to sit my father down when we returned to Canada where I would sift through his memories. My father and I would sit next to one another on the couch in his family room and engage in long conversations that were atypical of our relationship. I started by asking questions about my grandmother.

Only as soon as we began, I wished that I had asked the questions sooner, when my grandmother could have contributed to the answers. She adored her son and doted on me until the day her heart stopped working.

My grandma Earline was a big woman in more ways than one. She had wide, thick arms that she wrapped around me tightly as soon as she saw me. When we visited her in Ohio she would embrace me in a way that made me completely part of her—walled in by those immense arms and a body swollen with indulgences. I would listen to her heart race against my ear, drumming deep with affection from a love that was as large as she was.

On June 18, 1995, that embrace was left to memory when the cigarettes of her early days, the foods of Black America, a bout with diabetes, and her wonderful fullness all ganged up on her. My father discovered his mother on the floor of her apartment, face down, dead from a heart attack at age sixty-five. I was fourteen.

When my mother called from Ohio to deliver the news, I answered, five hours away in the suburbs of Toronto where I had finished my first year of high school. I didn't cry or ask questions. I just nodded as my mother relayed information. I tried to remember the important things I needed to pass along to my siblings.

Grandma's gone. Mom will call back later with more details.

Skye is older than I am by three years and when I called for her, she clambered down the stairs to my mother's country blue kitchen where the wallpaper was plastered with hearts that were the colour of Pepto Bismol. Skye sat down on a chair in the kitchen, and I delivered the news about Grandma. My sister's eyes turned red.

"How's Dad?" she asked, head lowered. Tears dripped onto her clasped fingers.

"Mom didn't say." Although I hadn't asked either.

Skye told me to call Damon. I picked up the phone and dialled the number that was posted on the refrigerator. Someone on the other end said they would go and get him. Skye leaned forward, elbows on the table, and stared out of the kitchen window.

"Hello?" Damon yelled.

I could hear the music and the noise of the party behind him, an indecipherable hum that grew louder. I held the top part of the phone away from my ear, the mouthpiece close to my lips.

"Damon? Damon, it's me."

"What?"

"It's Jael."

"Oh. Hey. What's up?" he yelled. I could hear him walking, the music fading.

"Grandma Earline died."

Skye looked over at me, eyes wide, but I turned away and ignored her exaggerated exhale and head shaking.

I heard the sound of a door closing, the background clear in the quiet. "Sorry?"

I took a deep breath.

"Mom just called. Grandma Earline had a heart attack. Dad found her."

Damon had been studying at the University of Toledo, where he was playing football at our father's alma mater—courageous, given our father's track record. He had recently come back to Canada for summer break. While he was in Toledo, he visited Grandma Earline every week, keeping her company while avoiding the homesickness that seemed to dissipate whenever he sat beside her watching Juke Box (a dial-in channel that played, by-request, popular and unheard-of eighties music videos) and eating pizza. Sometime later Damon would tell me that he knew Grandma Earline was dying every time they met—that she probably waited to go until he had left for the summer, because she wouldn't want her grandson to find her.

I'll never forget Damon's face when he got home from that party—a face that looked like mine, like our father's, only filled with pain and anger. Angry that he came home for the summer and left our grandmother alone; angry that I told him when he was at a party full of strangers, because he cried in front of them. Damon and Skye would explain all of the ways I handled things poorly, their tears falling steadily as I sat there straight-faced and tearless. I didn't quite get what was gone until later, but I would come to miss her desperately.

The thing I remember most about my grandmother, other than her embrace and the lip-puddle kisses she left on my cheek when we visited, were her homemade rolls. She made them for Thanksgiving dinners and Christmas holidays, and if we could convince her to make them for other occasions we did. But the task became too difficult in her later years. With every visit my mother warned, eyes round with admonition: *Do not ask about the rolls.*

She came to visit us in Canada when I was nine years old. I can still remember the smell of yeast and rising dough. I inhaled and filled my lungs and belly with a smell that seeped into my skin. I crept over to where she was working and watched masterful hand motions mix ingredients and shape each roll like pottery. Fingers gripped on the smooth curve of the counter, my heels pushed upwards, I peered over the ledge, eyes wide and hungry. She smiled suspiciously, and pointed a long, slender finger in my direction. *Do not eat the dough.*

I wanted to eat it because it smelled so good—because my nose and my mouth are inseparable friends that cannot keep secrets. She told me that if I ate the dough it would rise in my stomach until I exploded. This is what yeast does. Her face was serious. Is this possible? Can yeast make you explode? My siblings and I would debate this question for years.

When I asked my grandmother for the recipe, when I asked her to write it down, she told me to watch. That's what I did when I was your age, she said. But I didn't listen. I didn't watch. I didn't get it, and now I don't remember her hands—the ingredients her fingers rested on, how they shaped each roll: a handful of this, a pinch of that. I only remember the warning, the solemn expression, her pointy index. *Do not eat the dough.*

I've heard that when one sense stops working the others get stronger, sharper. When my grandmother died my senses felt dull—round and hollow like a spoon. So many things were lost when she died. So many things incomplete, left in want—the sense of smell, the sense of warmth, the sense of self.

People say I look like her, like that side of my family. You're your father's daughter, they say. You're an Ealey, that's for sure.

I just smile, nod politely. I have no idea what they mean by that. Is it because I have full thighs or curly hair? Is it because I laugh easily from deep in my belly, a cackle with a tooth-and-gum smile despite my best wishes? Because I see that in my father sometimes. I remember that about her.

My grandma Earline was the one person who could have told me everything. She was the one person who could have easily recalled what my father was like as a child, where her family came from and why they went to Portsmouth. In her absence I was left to piece together my family history from the memories of others—my father, my mother, and the people who knew our family in Portsmouth.

2

*A*LTHOUGH I have lived with my father most of my life, I didn't know anything about his childhood as I moved into adulthood. I didn't know any of his high school friends, where he hung out on weekends, or what his best and worst memories were. I had never even met my grandfather.

When I told my mother the kind of information I was looking for from my father, just before we left for Portsmouth, I could tell by her expression that she knew that extracting that information from him would be difficult, complicated. She knew I needed a head start if I was going to rely solely on my father's memory of things. She went to the wooden bedside table in the room she and my father shared, and then handed me a piece of paper from a basket of old papers and photos. It was something she had held onto since my grandmother died, something she showed me just then when I could better understand the context of the typewritten letters that appeared on my father's birth certificate.

Child's Name: Charles Ealey Jr.
Date of Birth: January 6, 1950
City of Birth: Portsmouth, Ohio
Mother of Child: Earline Pope Ealey

Mother's Age: Twenty
Mother's City of Birth: Superior, West Virginia
Race: Colored

I stared at it, read it over carefully. Her name was Earline Pope. She was from Superior, West Virginia. In 1950 she was *colored*.

"Your great-grandmother, Priscilla Pope, was originally from Bristol, Tennessee," my mother told me as I gripped the paper in my hand, as I ran my fingers along the worn texture and thought about the word *colored*.

I had never been to West Virginia, but I had visited the state of Tennessee—where my great-grandmother was raised—a few years earlier. I watched a man sell a ten-year-old boy a Confederate sword in the gift shop of the hotel where we were staying. The hotel was built inside an old train station. Is this your first Confederate sword? the storeowner asked the boy. The boy smiled, nodding exuberantly.

West Virginia, where my grandmother lived as a child, is northeast of Tennessee, squeezed between Ohio and the state of Virginia. Most of the state lies south of the Mason-Dixon—the imaginary line that historically separated America's free and slave states and splits West Virginia.

"Would West Virginia have been more like Ohio or Virginia back then?" I asked my parents from the hallway that separated the family room, where my father was sitting, from the kitchen, where my mother was doing dishes.

"Virginia," they said in unison.

"Is that why they left Superior? Is that why they went to Ohio?"

My mother shifted the dishes and pots she was washing, piling up items that banged and clanged and clinked against each other; I could tell by the way she pretended she hadn't heard me that this was beyond her scope of knowledge, so I walked into the family room and sat down on the couch next to my father.

"Dad?"

He angled his ear towards me, eyes on the TV. "Yup?"

"Why Portsmouth—where was your grandfather?"

He shrugged.

"Did you ever meet him? Did your grandmother ever mention him?"

"No," he said, I suppose to both questions.

Conversations with my father are always economical.

"I think he was dead," my father told me.

"You think he was dead before they left or—" I wasn't sure what to say, so I stopped, waited.

"I just assumed he was dead. Maybe they told me that, I don't know."

"You didn't ask them about him? Even when you were older?"

He looked over at me, perturbed or perplexed. I couldn't figure out exactly what he was thinking.

I sat there next to my father in silence and thought about Priscilla Pope and her three children in the forties in Superior, West Virginia. I imagined my great-grandmother packing their belongings, standing inside a small, rundown apartment—a few clothes in a few small pieces of luggage. She must have felt tired, heavy. She must have thought of her home in Tennessee. Why was she moving further away, with three children? It must have been her only choice, the best solution to her problems. *I've got to get out of here. I've got to find someplace safer, different.* Alberta and James, the two eldest, would have sensed the worry and concern, felt the danger. I imagine they would have tried to be strong, helpful, hopeful. They would have admired her courage. But my grandma Earline—just eleven years old at the time and, like me, the youngest—would have thought of what might lie ahead, seen the adventure. She would imagine that kids in Ohio were kinder than they were in West Virginia, that things would get better—maybe people in Ohio wouldn't spit in her hair, point, laugh, call her Fat Nigger. This is what my grandmother must have thought about as she looked out of the bus window, crammed in the back among distraught black faces, on the journey that brought her from Superior, West Virginia, to Portsmouth, Ohio.

When I was in middle school, my father accepted a job out in Richmond Hill, a Toronto suburb that was over an hour's drive from where we lived in Mississauga. He had been given a promotion and he wanted us to move to a neighbourhood near his new office. My brother was starting university, but my sister and I would both be in high school. My sister would have to transfer to a brand new secondary school, and I would have to go to a high school far away from the ones my friends in middle school were planning on attending. My father asked if the move was okay with us, and my sister and I thought about it—new schools, new sports teams, new best friends, new in-crowds. Change had never been our forte. We would rather stay in Mississauga, we said.

"I'll be away a lot," my father explained to us.

We just nodded. It must have hurt him to see us choose our friends over him so unanimously, so quickly. It must have hurt him to watch us sacrifice his presence for our convenience. When I think about what would happen between us when he was gone so regularly, I often think about the choice he gave us. It's the tricky thing about privilege, choices. Given the choice, most of us choose what's easier, more convenient. Most big things, like the move my grandmother made at thirteen and what unfolded for my father, happen when there are few, if any, choices.

My best friend in middle school was Lorraine West, who I met a few years earlier at a summer Bible program when we were eleven. Her skin was smooth and dark, and she had full lips that she began to slather with deep-red lipsticks, when we started to attend middle school together. In grade eight we ran into the first of many problems that would cause our friendship to slowly deteriorate, until issues of race would irreparably divide us.

Lorraine was the oldest of three and lived in a townhouse, where she shared a room with her sister. She was charged with taking care of both her siblings throughout the summer. Lorraine's family was Jamaican and regularly had big barbecues with other black, Christian families; my family attended an all-white church in a small nearby town.

In grade eight, Lorraine and I made friends with a girl named Rae Levine, who was also Jamaican. She had caramel-brown skin and light eyes, but she and Lorraine both possessed the same confidence about themselves and their blackness, a sensibility I lacked entirely. They understood reggae lyrics and wore colourful T-shirts with black cartoon characters. T-shirts that read: "2 Black, 2 Beautiful" and "Sisterhood," with matching bright-coloured shoelaces. I tried to dress like the girls in the Gap commercials I saw on television.

Rae had a full chest and a stocky build, and balled her fists at the first sign of trouble. She never backed down from a fight or even lost one. She kissed her teeth and backtalked teachers when they did something she didn't agree with. No boy or girl wanted to mess with her. Rae's sister had just been released from juvenile detention that year, according to rumours. Rae was a rough-and-tumble convict by association.

"I don't trust her. Lorraine should watch out," I told a friend one day when I started to feel on the outside of our new three-way friendship. Rae and Lorraine had begun laughing together more about things I didn't understand; they hung around together after school while I was at volleyball practice. Her sister was in *prison*, I whispered to others.

A few days later, Rae, Lorraine, and Rae's juvenile delinquent sister appeared in the window of the doors to the gym where

I was practising. I could see their eyes peering in, fingers pointing in my direction. I concentrated on having soft hands, bending my knees, spiking the ball, and blocking with stiff hands and spread fingers. Rae's sister was enrolled at the high school next door to our middle school. She was rail thin and had a small, narrow face and bulgy, green eyes that I recognized right away through the glass of the gymnasium door. She was searching like a hungry amphibian.

I took the back doors out of the gym after practice to get my school bag, past the garbage heap, the lost and found pile, and the ramp to the school stage, then up the stairs to my second floor locker. As I fiddled with the locker combination, I heard footsteps in the empty hallway. I packed my bag, closed my locker and headed back down the stairs, but Rae and her sister caught up to me and pulled me into the girls' washroom. Lorraine followed in behind them.

They asked me if what they had heard was true. Had I said that they were trouble? Had I said that they were dangerous criminals? My back was up against a brick wall. The sisters were standing in front of me waiting for an answer, their green eyes fixed on me. I knew the story had made its way back to Lorraine, that she was their informant. I could see it in her guilty silence, the way she avoided eye contact.

"Nope, I never said that. Why would I say that?"

I could tell they didn't believe me. I could also tell that this was not the right time to point out the irony—the truth of my grapevine-heard statements. I closed my eyes and started to imagine what my face would look like in shades of blue and purple. Lorraine just stood there behind the two sisters, moderately fearful.

A teammate stepped into the washroom and yelled that my mother was waiting out front for me. I used the opportunity to escape the Levines' fists of punishment. I ran between the sisters and Lorraine, and out of the washroom. I ran all the way down the hall until I was seated and buckled in my mother's minivan. I said to my mother through my tears, Skye seated in the front: I want to move to Richmond Hill. I want to go to a different high school. Only it was too late.

For the next few years my father left the house at six in the morning, Monday through Friday. I would hear him pass my door while I pretended to sleep. He would climb down the steps and walk into the kitchen where he would pour himself a cup of coffee. I would listen for the heavy swing of the door to the garage before I got up. On a good day, he came back fourteen hours later. Sometimes he stayed overnight, or for a series of nights, at a hotel near his office building. On weekends he would sleep and hibernate in front of the TV or in the basement, tired from work and the hectic city driving.

My father and I would pass each other in the house during these years in ways that indicated mere acquaintanceship: cordial hellos, minimalist banter, intermittent conversations. It wasn't until I went to Portsmouth and stood by my grandfather's gravesite, that I understood how my relationship with my father reflected history.

3

I N MY SECOND YEAR of university, when I was newly twenty, I took a course called Black America. My professor, Dr. Clarence Munford, was a man of cinematic presence. He rarely smiled but he was never angry. His hair was salted with wisdom, experience lined in the wrinkles of his face. He was black, in a way that I admired, not only because his skin was the colour of wet earth, but because he understood history—all its weights and pleasures. He carried his blackness in the straightness of his back, across the breadth of his shoulders. I envied how he walked into a room, and with one breath, conveyed that proud sensibility.

Dr. Munford was the first person to introduce me to black history, to the realities of my father's childhood and the residue of slavery. He taught with a precision and devotion I admired and envied. He told me what happened and when, and where he was during all of it. When I was a boy, he would say, as he filled my mind with history.

His class focused on the impact of slavery on the black community today, on the gaps in the Emancipation Proclamation, on the civil rights movement, and on the significant events of the sixties and seventies. He taught us about segregation, the riots in

1960 and 1964, the upheaval that followed Dr. King's assassination in 1968. He told me what American men were experiencing at the time, what they were witnessing in the newspapers and on television—depression and desperation, abuse by police, rejection. I recorded each word vigorously, did the math for each of those historic civil uprisings—my father would have been ten in 1960, fourteen in 1964, eighteen and starting college in 1968. From the back of Dr. Munford's class I sat and wondered why I didn't know about any of it.

When my father and mother bought a new home that backed onto a golf course in a neighbourhood of three-car garages, my father finished the basement with an array of sports memorabilia. Signed hockey jerseys, pictures of famous golfers, a framed collection of Super Bowl tickets—all hung on the walls near the big-screen TV around the air hockey, foosball, and pool tables. It was my father's haven, his retreat. When he had parties or celebrated big events, he gladly welcomed visitors to his retreat.

When a documentary about his football career was almost complete in 2008, my father invited family and friends over to watch the trailer. We watched the statistics, awards, and key points of my father's life flash in a collection of camera shots and old photographs, slimmed-down quotes from famous friends: coaches, players, sportswriters. An image of my grandmother, arm around my father when he looked to be about six, appeared on the screen.

"*Chuck Ealey was raised in a small home in the projects,*" the narrator's voice said.

It had been so long since I had seen my grandmother, so rare to see a picture of them together when she was so young and my father was a child. My stomach turned.

"*Earline Ealey had only a grade eight education . . .*"

I looked around at my siblings, at my mother, all watching as the trailer went on.

"*She raised him with—*"

Wait. Stop. Grade eight? *Grade eight?*

I thought of my grandmother squinting at her pill bottles, the scribbled lines of her signature on my Christmas cards. I thought of the way she made those rolls, the recipes she never wrote down because it was a family recipe, the way she encouraged me to watch, remember. Someone should have told me.

"Why didn't she stay in school?" I asked my father the next day, when we were seated at the kitchen table. I would have watched her make those rolls. I would have written down the recipe. I would have done things differently.

"Dad?"

My father was reading a newspaper, my mother preparing breakfast. He rested his mug on the table, his forehead wrinkled. "There weren't a lot of options back then," he said.

I couldn't tell if he was disappointed or offended by the question. I waited for him to lecture me, to say something, to explain, but he just took a sip of coffee and went back to reading his newspaper.

My first job, age twelve, was delivering newspapers after school, three days a week. I wanted a cherry-red wagon like kids on TV had. Only my parents refused to buy me one.

"You can use the wheelbarrow," my father said.

Our wheelbarrow was an orange-rust colour with oak handles and brown spots where the edges had nicked brick, where shovels had chipped away parts of the basin.

"You can save up for a wagon," he said.

I was saving up for a Walkman that was see-through and red, from Consumers Distributing, so I could listen to my favourite cassette whenever I wanted—Whitney Houston's *I Want to Dance With Somebody*. I thought about the album cover each time I pushed that rust wheelbarrow: brown happy face, wild curly hair like mine, white tank top, brilliant teeth.

I wobbled newspapers door-to-door for two months until I had earned enough money. Then I went to Consumers Distributing, and bought the Walkman from a catalogue. Then I quit my job. The newspapers made my hands black, especially when it rained, and delivering newspapers out of a wheelbarrow was embarrassing. Truth is, once I had Whitney and my Walkman, there was no reason to suffer through any more of it.

My father told me that my grandmother never enrolled in school after moving to Portsmouth because she needed to help the family. She cleaned houses and ironed clothes for white people, starting at the age of thirteen; she eventually accepted a position as a nurse's aide in Portsmouth's local hospital.

"She was treated well, from what I remember," he said as my mother pushed the jaws of the waffle iron down, batter squishing out the sides, strips of bubbling bacon popping in a pan. "She was respected. She was never abused or mistreated. It was a good job at the time," he told me.

In 1943, my grandmother was thirteen. She was black and poor, tall, already heavy. She ironed clothes and cleaned toilets, while white kids her age went to school. She cleaned up blood and waste while white doctors did rounds so they could send their kids to good colleges. Sacrificing education was common among black people who lived in segregated neighbourhoods that were affluent with poverty. It was not the only issue, however, that would complicate my father's childhood.

4

Y GRANDMOTHER and her sister Alberta (who had Alzheimer's for as long as I knew her) were the only people I knew from my father's family, until a woman's phone call, when I was ten years old, made me aware of the wide range of things my father hadn't shared about his life in Portsmouth.

Woman: Is Junior there, please?

Me: There's no one here by that name.

Woman: Is this Chuck's daughter?

Me: Yes. *But who's Junior?*

My father's name is Charles Ealey Jr. because he is the second Charles Ealey in the family. He is referred to as Junior in the area where he grew up, because he is named after a man who I heard about for the first time when a woman named Norma Jean called our house to speak with Junior.

Six years later, in 1997, Norma Jean called again to deliver important news about Charles Ealey Sr. My grandfather was dying. My father packed his bags. I begged him to take me with him. *Please. Let me come.*

I'm losing myself. This is how I felt, age sixteen, triggered by the mention of a dying man I didn't know. *I'm losing my sense of blackness.* I was being told in both words and expressions by people both black and white: *You're not really black.* I didn't talk right or look right or fit in with the right people. Maybe they were right. I was missing something—a sense of where I came from. If I could see my grandfather, perhaps I could recover the part of me that felt like it was missing.

My grandmother was gone and so were her rolls, her smell, her full presence. But my grandfather was still here. He was a man I didn't know, wouldn't recognize, couldn't describe as tall, short, skinny, or smart. He was part of me and I wanted to know him, wanted to touch his skin while it was still warm and marked with memories. It was my last chance to untangle his story— to speak to the man who helped give him life and to ask him my questions. What did you witness, touch, know? Please, tell me.

Please, Dad. Let me come.

This is what I cried alone in my room while my father was on his way to Portsmouth.

When my father returned from Portsmouth that July in 1997, after my grandfather passed away, he didn't say much about what happened, and I was angry. My father had deliberately kept me from knowing his father and he wouldn't even explain his reasons. He wouldn't talk about my grandfather or show me a picture. The only thing I had from my grandfather was what my father brought home from the funeral.

It was an American flag folded in a triangle and held inside plastic like the sandwiches my mother packed in Ziplocs when I was in elementary school. It was wrapped tightly with careful precision, rich red stripes tucked neatly behind a blue patch covered in stars that were dull white like potatoes. My mother placed it on a shelf in our family room because it matched the navy and red décor.

I looked at that flag often, studied it, took in the symbols of patriotism portrayed through the plastic. Until one day when I went looking for something tangible deep inside the contents.

I stepped onto the seat cushions of the pilled brown couch that was placed perpendicular to the bookshelf—one foot pressed into the arm rest, the other foot on the ledge, my body stretching upwards against the honey-coloured shelving that stretched up to the ceiling. I pinched the corner of the plastic with the tips of my fingers and slid the package towards me, the bronze shell casings clanging as the package fell against me.

I sat down on the couch and traced the angled edges of the package with my finger. I undid the zipper and stuck my hand in, rubbed the thick, bumpy fabric, touched the coolness of the metal casings from the five-gun salute. I pressed my nose into the open package, searching for something—the scent of fresh grass, smoked gunpowder, my grandfather's aftershave. Only I couldn't smell anything.

When my friends saw the flag in the family room when I was in high school, I told them the only thing I knew at the time, based on what my mother had told me: It's my grandfather's. He was a soldier. He fought in World War II. I think I made him sound like a hero because they just stared and nodded. They always found it impressive. Only when my father heard me say this, he huffed and didn't say anything.

On our visit to Portsmouth in 2008, my father took us on a tour of the town. We drove down streets as my father pointed out local landmarks: the donut store, the public high school, the cemetery. My mother sat in the front seat, my brother and I in the back with my five-year-old nephew between us.

"That's where your grandfather is buried," my father said.

"Can we take a look?" I said, eyes fixed on the iron rod fence that bordered the cemetery.

"Why?" my father said.

"Because. Because, I want to go."

My father said nothing.

"Dad, can we go? Please."

"No."

I had trouble explaining to my father why I wanted to know about my grandfather. Mentioning him always made my father's jaw tighten. I thought that if I stood by his grave, I could figure out what my father wasn't able to tell me.

My mother stared at my father from the passenger seat beside him. He looked up at me in the mirror, then over at my mother. Just give her what she wants, Chuck. My father exhaled and manoeuvred the car down a twisted driveway towards an area filled with rows of identical, small, white headstones—hundreds in perfect neat lines that circled around a monument, peeking out from the long blades of grass and bundled flowers.

Approximately 125,000 black men enlisted in the U.S. Armed Forces in the 1940s, back when the military was still segregated. Black soldiers were separated from white soldiers for church services and transportation; their canteens were kept separate from the ones used by white soldiers.

As I wove between the rows of headstones, I thought about the irony. These men hadn't worshipped together or shared water. Now their differences were indecipherable, buried under a blanket of grass and mounds of dirt.

"It's somewhere around here," my father said.

My brother and I walked along the rows, weaving in and out, until we spotted a name that we recognized: *Charles Ealey Sr., TEC 5, US ARMY, WORLD WAR II, January 6, 1919—July 28, 1997.*

We stopped for a moment, inhaled quickly.

"You have the same birthday," I said.

My father nodded.

"Did you know that—did you know you were born on the same day?" I asked him.

My father shrugged. I watched him for a moment, his skin a dark summer brown, his eyes the same deep black as mine but different, fixed on something distant.

I looked at his face and tried to guess what he was thinking. There was no hint of loss or resentment on his face, as we stood next to my grandfather's grave. There was no remorse or anger. Just an expression that typified apathy.

I met my father's friend, Al Bass, at a football game just after our visit to my grandfather's grave. Al had lived in the North End and had also come back to Portsmouth for homecoming weekend. He was tall, broad-shouldered, full of charm, and brimming with memories of life in the segregated projects. I asked him about his work at the college where he was an administrator, about a hurricane that was making its way to his neighbourhood in Texas. Eventually we got to talking about what it was that had brought me to Portsmouth.

"Did you know my grandparents?"

"Of course I knew your grandparents," he said. "Everybody knows everybody here. Your grandmother was a lovely woman. Lovely."

I smiled and nodded as Al turned to the game, watched the wrinkles on his head roll and pucker as his eyes roamed the field, following the football. He looked down into the cup he was holding, lowered his voice.

"Your grandfather was an alcoholic," he said. "He had a lot of problems."

Al and I kept our eyes on the game as Al shared about his own broken home, of the father he never knew in Portsmouth.

He was trying to make me feel better, because he could see my disappointment over the news of Chuck Senior—which is what Al called him.

"None of the boys from the North End lived with their fathers," Al said.

He explained that some of the men in the North End knew who their fathers were and some knew where they were (jail, the cemetery, another woman's home). I came to discover that because of his name and notoriety, my father always knew both when it came to his father.

"I lived in the same city and I knew who my father was, but there was no real relationship," my father told me when we were back in Canada, when I asked him about what Al Bass told me about his father.

My father told me that Chuck Senior worked in construction as a brick mason. He was known as a rambler and got into a lot of trouble on account of his drinking—a habit that escalated when he returned from the war.

"What do you remember about him?" I asked.

"Not a whole lot, because he wasn't there. The things I remember were probably the negative things." My father shifted his weight, adjusted the pillow behind him. "Something came back to me just recently that I remember," he said. "He and my mom were getting a divorce. I remember I was taken to the court-house and they asked me to come up to the witness box so I could tell them who I wanted to live with. I saw my dad coming in the courtroom, but then he turned around and left. I don't know whether he was late. Maybe he knew that I was going to say I wanted to live with my mother." My father stopped and shrugged. "That was basically it. I don't recall anything as a kid other than my mother and grandmother getting me raised."

I tried to imagine what that would feel like—to have to choose between the man you were named after and your mother as a five-year-old boy. It must have been traumatic, terrifying. Only my father spoke about it the same way he handled all of his memories—with simplicity and detachment.

"My dad drank a lot. I mean *a lot*. He was shot and stabbed. He should have been dead a couple times," my father said, coolly.

"Shot and stabbed?" I said. "Doing what?"

"When I was a kid, he got into an argument with another man, and he was stabbed. The guy took a knife to his stomach, and it should have killed him because the stab mark was right around his navel. I do remember that. I remember that as a kid I couldn't go into the hospital room, but I could be lifted up to the window. I waved at him. I must have been six or seven."

"And he was shot too?"

My father propped his glasses on top of his head and then squinted towards the ceiling, trying to remember where he was at the time, whether or not he was in university or if it happened when he was living in Canada.

"I remember that," my mother shouted from the kitchen. "We were married. Someone from Ohio called. Norma Jean, maybe? Chuck Senior had been shot. He'd been shot by some woman, remember?"

My father huffed and shook his head, a laugh that was short and uncomfortable.

"Yeah, that's right. He was shot by some woman."

That was all they could remember about my grandfather's other near-death encounter.

My grandfather was in his late seventies when my father's half-sister Norma Jean called for the last time regarding Chuck Senior. He doesn't have a lot of time, was what she told him.

"There was a growth underneath his heart the size of a tennis ball," my father told me. "He was really sick—the tumour was affecting him. He couldn't talk but he was trying to tell us something. It was about the money."

I tilted my head, wrinkled skin just over the bridge of my nose.

"I never told you about the money?" my father said.

I shook my head.

"He had some money in the house but he hid it. He hid it in a cookie jar. Two thousand dollars in cash. It was supposed to be for his burial. He was worried someone would steal it. He knew he was dying and he couldn't tell us where it was because he was so sick. He was getting frustrated, but I figured it out. Norma Jean sent her son to tidy up the house; he found the money during the clean-up. I covered the other costs."

There was no apology, no final message for his Canadian grandchildren. Just his concern for the amount of money he had saved up for his burial.

The fact that Chuck Senior left my father an outstanding bill on his deathbed was sadly ironic. In the thirty years that would transpire between my father's birth in 1950 and my own Canadian arrival in 1980, everything would change for my father and our family, in spite of my grandfather. My father would pay off more than a funeral bill. He would pay off the life-debt Chuck Senior had passed down to him. He would circumvent a history of poverty and abandonment.

5

WHEN I was younger, I often tried to imagine my father as a child or a teenager, but it always stumped me. He seems to have been born an adult. Even in his childhood pictures, a deep maturity is evident. Was he ever wild or reckless? I wondered. Did he ever disobey, rebel, or sneak out after curfew? Or was he always reliable and responsible? Did he always make good choices? It's why I was so excited to meet his classmates at his fortieth high school reunion in Portsmouth.

I knew very little about his life at Notre Dame High School. I thought that if I could see them, if I could ask them questions about those days, if I could watch his interactions with them, I would understand a different part of my father.

I made plans to listen carefully and ask pointed questions, as we headed towards a party at the house of a classmate named Mary Barry.

The sunset sky was vibrant with colours that striped between the hills and across the farmlands that surrounded the highway into Portsmouth. Damon and my nephew stayed back at the hotel, while my father, my mother, and I all headed towards the party where the Class of '68 had already begun the celebrations.

"Hi, Mary Barry," my father said into his cellphone, as we headed up a steep hill.

Mary was the social convenor for the homecoming reunion weekend. She had married another classmate, so she was no longer Mary Barry, but my father continued to refer to her that way and I did the same.

"Yes, we're coming . . . I have your address. Sherri and my youngest are coming."

My father laughed for a moment over something Mary said before repeating my name, *Ja-el, Jay-ell*. She probably thought that it was just two initials. I had been getting that all my life. It was the first time I realized that my father had to explain it just as much as I did.

"What kind of name is that?" people would say to me.

"Hebrew. It's from the Bible."

"Really?"

"It's in Judges. She kills a wicked king by drilling a tent peg through his head with a hammer."

I always smiled when I said that, because it's one of those great, unknown stories about a woman of character, wit, and fearlessness.

It was quiet when we got out of the car—hot and buggy. My father led the way towards the house, dogs barking and crickets chirping around us. He opened the door to an unlit screened-in porch and stepped into a kitchen filled with bags of chips, paper plates, and stacks of linked hot dog buns wrapped in clear plastic. A pot of pulled pork bubbled on the stovetop.

A woman screamed "Chuck!" in a thick southern Ohio accent that made his name rhyme with *deck* instead of *duck*.

"Mary!"

My father and Mary embraced. *This is Mary Barry?*

People poured out from behind walls and through all of the entryways, until we were surrounded, my father's name on everyone's lips—my father hugged and welcomed like the prodigal son. There were low bellows from teammates and squeals from wives and former classmates. I looked around. *They're all white.*

"You remember Sherri," my father said after Mary hugged him.

"Of course," said Mary.

"Hi, Mary," my mother said as they embraced.

"Hi, Sherri."

"Good to see you." "When was the last time?" chimed voices.

My mother turned and spoke with a woman who had made her way forward. All eyes turned to me.

"This is my youngest daughter, Jael," my father said.

"Hi." I prayed I had said this out loud, or that the brief wave that accompanied my greeting would be sufficient, because I was standing there in that kitchen living inside my head, trying to process all that I was seeing.

Introductions followed: This is Mary Barry (white), Mike Winkler (white), Tom Danini (white). People appeared from various corners of the house. In the chaos they self-introduced. I'm John. I'm Alice. I played ball with your dad (white, white, white).

Classmates, spouses, and more classmates all came into the kitchen from the family room. They came in from the porch area to welcome us. But I lost most of the names after Mary. I tried to appear nonchalant, dug through my memory while they smiled, shook my hand, told me I had a pretty name. "What does J.L. stand for?" they asked. I was flabbergasted.

After we left the party, I climbed in the car and slammed the door. "You didn't tell me your classmates were white!"

When I was in university, a Disney movie came out about an integrated football team in Mississippi. As we were watching it, my father said: "That was like my high school." When he said this, when he threw it at me in passing, I thought he meant that his school was integrated, that it wasn't an all-black high school like I would have imagined, given what I knew of the North End. I thought there were still a lot of black kids. What I didn't know until that night was that there were only a few kids from the North End at Notre Dame High School—just two others in addition to my dad in the Class of '68, neither of whom made it to the party at Mary Barry's.

When I looked at my father in the rear-view mirror after the party and waited for an explanation, my father just shrugged and said, as though it explained everything, "I went to a Catholic school."

That didn't explain anything. In Canada, Catholic schools meant that the Bible was allowed to be spoken of by teachers, that prayer was acceptable, that Jesus, Mary, and a Creator-God were okay words to use in discussions, and that kids had to wear a uniform. There were Muslims and Christians and atheists who went there—brown kids and black kids and white ones. Some went for the moral standards, some the uniforms. Others went because it was the closest school to their home.

When I got back to the hotel that night, I woke up my brother and said, "They were white, Damon. They were *all* white."

Damon was as surprised as I was, because he knew it changed everything. It meant it wasn't weird that all of our parents' friends in Canada were white. It wasn't odd that my father got his hair done by an Italian hairdresser instead of a black barber. It meant my father and I weren't as different as I thought.

The high school my siblings and I attended in Mississauga was a zoo—different types of animals forced to live together in confined, constricted spaces; some lurking in corners, some on rocks, some wading suspiciously in algae-infested waters. Zoos are divided into geographic regions. So was my high school cafeteria.

By the time I attended Meadowvale Secondary School, I had been in the cafeteria a number of times on account of my sister and brother. But in grade nine, I was no longer a visitor. I stood in the doorway on my first lunch period and waited, searching through the squeals and the roars and the raucous noise—searching for my region.

Throughout the cafeteria were long, metal bench tables—evenly distributed in rows, lined up in columns like the seats in a jumbo jet. Near the main doors, which were brown and steel, was the First Table. It was located in prime position, en route to the vending machines and the cafeteria servery, in full view of the school entrance, the front foyer, and the main office. It was closest to the door and easiest to get to, and by virtue of a not-so-subtle social expectation of occupation, it was dominated and permanently inhabited by the black students.

I stood in the doorway at lunchtime on my first day of high school—watching, waiting, vulnerable. A boy at the First Table swirled and swivelled dominoes across the surface of the table like ice cubes. When he stopped, he and three other boys picked up the small rectangles, until the table was empty and each boy had the same amount of tiles gripped between their fingers and tilted upwards. They read them like books, peering at the tiles in careful analysis. One boy slid a tile into the centre. The boys took turns placing tiles down, one to another.

Nestled in among the rest of the group at the First Table, wearing a tight, brown-striped, legging-dress combo that revealed her navel, was my best friend, Lorraine West. I waited until she saw me. We made eye contact and she waved me over, then moved to make room for me. I sat down in the seat she vacated while she climbed into the lap of a male student. I watched out of the corner of my eye as the boy wrapped his arms around her and placed his hands casually on the thickest part of her thigh. She slapped his hand, laughing coyly.

SMACK! One of the boys in the game slammed a domino against the First Table so the tiles bounced and rattled, shaking out of their geometric, snake structure. He stood and bellowed words I didn't understand, and everyone at the First Table laughed and celebrated exuberantly. Around the cafeteria, white faces stared back at me, at us, their expressions confirming what I felt, but what I would try desperately to hide for the rest of the year. I was in the wrong zoogeographic region.

"Where are you from?" one of the boys asked one day, as I sat at the First Table.

"I'm Canadian."

"Where are your parents from?"

"They're American."

"But where are they *from*?"

"America."

"Like, before that?"

"Before the boat that brought them from Africa?"

Nobody liked that answer.

The students at the First Table were from the Caribbean. They knew about hardo bread and bun and cheese and dominoes—a game that involves matching like-numbered tiles and reading the moves of other players. A game that is always played loudly. They were from large islands and small ones and ate roti and curried goat and flying fish for lunch, while I brought cold-cut subs, peanut butter sandwiches, and leftover pizza. At the First Table I learned that peas didn't come in Jolly Green Giant cans or sit bold and green next to your white rice; they were red or brown and they were mixed into rice that was fluffy, dense, and filling.

The black students at the First Table wore their countries' names and flags on their T-shirts, hats, earrings, and fingernails. They were so certain of their ancestry and their place in the world, that in their presence I felt particularly deficient in blackness.

"What are *body riders*?" I said to a friend after a story was told about a girl who was wearing them that day (as far as I could decipher).

Those who overheard repeated my pronunciation, laughing hysterically.

"It's *bahtee ridahs*," they told me.

When my red face and searching eyes revealed I still didn't get it, they laughed even harder. *Bahtee ridahs* was not a term you could anglicise.

I knew *bahtee ridahs* by a term that was used on an American television series about two white cowboys, and their bombshell cousin Daisy who made tiny shorts iconic. Besides, "Daisy Dukes" was easier for me to pronounce.

As time went by in high school, Lorraine came to look more and more like the women on the covers of my grandmother's *Jet* magazines. She became increasingly curvy in the hips and wore outfits that hugged her silhouette.

Lorraine permed her hair straight, her kinky curls carefully disciplined by way of an intricate set of chemicals, hair dryers, and treatments. She kept it long, glistened with hair oils. At night, she wrapped her head in a scarf to maintain the straightness. For important occasions, she would sleep sitting up or dangle her head off the edge of her bed to retain her hairdo perfection. Other black girls always commented on her stylish do's and how healthy it looked, despite the chemicals.

Even though her hair was the subject of much praise, whenever I was around and the hair topic erupted, Lorraine would look at me with longing tinged with resentment. She would pull on a ringlet and say that I had good hair. You are lucky, she would tell me. I would smile, full of discomfort, as I tucked my curl back into its place among the others.

Lorraine began to don green, yellow, and black in increas-
ing excess in high school. She wore medallions, colourful earrings, shoelaces, and T-shirts covered in Jamaican yellow X's.
She began to speak with an accent when the First Table students
made jokes about their West Indian parents—their "good china",
their marinated chicken, their insistence on ground provisions
like yams and potatoes, or whether they used a stick or one of
daddy's belts to discipline unruly children. As I listened to stories
about their households, homes that were far different from my
own, I just tried to smile and laugh at the same time Lorraine did.

I said as little as possible during that first year of high school,
in order to avoid embarrassment or a repeat of the *bahtee ridahs*
disaster. I lived in an atypical quiet until I entered my second
year at Meadowvale.

In grade ten, I was placed in the enriched program—an academic distinction based on standardized testing. There were a
few Asian students in the program, but the majority of my classmates were white. Like the teenybopper TV shows I watched on
Saturday mornings, I was the only black person. I don't know if
it was a racist allotment or happenstance, but Lorraine would
claim the former because she was a good student who was not
selected for the program. She was despondent about the change,
but I was hopeful. Maybe this distinction could help me solid-
ify friendships where I could be more authentic—where Canadian was a suitable answer to the where-are-you-from question,
where I wasn't the only person who would never be able to say
bahtee ridahs in a way that sounded natural.

My new high school friends came from this class—a group of
boys who loved sports and an entourage of girls who loved those
same boys. The group expanded in subsequent years to include a
baseball player named Shaan, whose parents were from Pakistan
(the only other person of any kind of colour), Dan Noble who

played on the football team, and other athletes and sports fans who shared our interests. Lorraine and I would see less and less of one another. For the remainder of high school I would spend my lunches at the nearby mall instead of the high school cafeteria.

I'm not sure why I felt like I belonged among this group—I stood out among its members more than I ever did at the First Table. Perhaps it's because our differences were clear to everyone who saw us, not isolated inside my own discomfort. Among this new group, there wasn't the same requirement to be black enough.

When Homer Plessy, one-eighth black and seven-eighths white, was jailed on June 7, 1892, for sitting in the "white" car on the East Louisiana Railroad, Plessy argued that the Separate Car Act—which required him to sit in a car designated for blacks— violated his Thirteenth and Fourteenth Amendment rights. The U.S. Supreme Court decided that although the Separate Car Act was "unconstitutional on trains that travel through several states," the state of Louisiana's decision should be upheld so long as the train operated within state borders.

The case established a critical precedent that would pose significant challenges for black citizens in post-emancipation America. Separate facilities for blacks and whites were deemed legal, so long as they were equal. The decision formed the basis for legalized segregation. White Americans would focus on *separate* with little concern for *equal* standards of cleanliness or access, as outlined in the decision. Offices, restaurants, theatres, and businesses would post signs in prominent and well-maintained sections of their facilities, signs which read or implied: Whites Only.

Black Americans and activists would work to bring an end to segregation in the fifties and sixties in particular. Their efforts would focus on two key strategies: 1) overturn the Supreme Court's 1896, *Plessy v. Ferguson* decision; 2) mobilize Americans to support the cause across the country through protests, marches, and demonstrations. Their endeavours became known as the civil rights movement.

On May 17, 1954, in the famous case of *Brown v. Board of Education*, civil rights activists would accomplish something important. The Supreme Court declared all laws that supported segregated schools unconstitutional. The government called for the desegregation of schools across the nation. In accordance with the new mandate, nine black students started to attend the previously all-white Little Rock Central High School in Arkansas in 1952—a state known for its resistance to desegregation and the civil rights movement. The students were harassed on their way to school and verbally abused throughout their time at Little Rock Central.

Less than a decade after those events made national headlines, my father walked to school with two black friends from the segregated projects in Portsmouth, Ohio, to attend Notre Dame Catholic High School.

I shifted my feet on the linoleum tiles as Mike Winkler leaned up against the counter in Mary Barry's kitchen. He stood nearly six and a half feet, with a rounded belly, a giant in size and personality. He reminded me of my own former classmates back in Canada—the beer, the good humour, the sport-centred conversation. When the crowd in the kitchen had thinned out to a handful of people, he was the first person I asked about my father. Mike had been a wide receiver for the Notre Dame Titans.

"If I didn't catch his passes, he never would have made it. He got my scholarship! I should have gone to UT. Chuck couldn't have made it to UT without me," Winkler said.

Everyone laughed, including Winkler.

"Seriously," he said. "Ask Mary."

"Well, I'm just not so sure about that, Mike," Mary said as she turned to me with a wide grin. "But it was a team effort."

"Academically it was a team effort."

This came from John. He was the class genius. He didn't play on the football team but he could recall from memory my father's football statistics.

"Was he a good student?" I said.

Mary nodded, hesitant. "Yeah. He was a good student."

"You tutored him," Winkler said to Mary.

"He needed some help?" I looked around, but no one said anything.

I had never thought of my father performing below average or under expectation in anything. I had never thought of him struggling academically. I thought of all of the sales awards that were dusty in storage, all of his trophies and accomplishments, about the times when I brought home nineties and he asked me about the ten per cent that was missing. I didn't get prizes for getting straight A's. I worked for them because I never wanted to know what my father would say if I didn't perform well in school.

Mary Barry shrugged her shoulders. "We had tough teachers."

The conversation turned to a collection of old high school newspapers Mary had spread out on the dining room table. Later in the evening Mary said to me, eyes solemn, voice low in reflective confession, "He's in financial planning and I helped him in math."

I thought about the comments made by Mike Winkler and about Mary's tutorials when I read a report sometime later that was written by a United States government official about the conditions affecting "American Negroes" around the time my father was in high school:

There is absolutely no question of any genetic differential: Intelligence potential is distributed among Negro infants in the same proportion as among Icelanders or Chinese or any other group. American society, however, impairs the Negro potential.

It hinted at what I would discover over the course of the week-end and through conversations with my father when I was back in Canada. Although riddled with problems that reflected the times, attending Notre Dame—where my father buffed the floors every summer to pay his tuition—significantly altered his story.

Coach Ed Miller was the football, basketball, and track and field coach at Notre Dame High School when my father started there in 1964. My father's classmates from Notre Dame told me that he ran an authoritarian athletic regime and wore a militant expression. It earned him the moniker Coach Smiley.

During summer training, Coach Miller made his players take salt pills and withheld water to teach them mental toughness. When the team manager felt unbearably sorry for the pitifully parched athletes, he would soak a towel in water and sneak it out on the field when a player went down and Coach Miller wasn't looking. In a secretive huddle of dire thirst, the boys would suck on the towel to collect small slurps of refreshment.

"He'd be in prison now for what he did," Winkler said. "But the reason we won everything was because we were trained like Navy SEALs."

When my father was in his second year of high school, Coach Miller put him in for a few plays in the quarterback position to relieve starter Pete O'Malley. My father had a good arm—strong, precise and accurate from those stone-throwing days by the train tracks. He could also run the ball—a trait Coach Miller relished in a quarterback. In the fall of 1966, Pete O'Malley was moved to tight end, and my father became the Notre Dame Titans' starting quarterback.

"Every Monday after the game, the coaches would come into the change room and announce the Player of the Week. It was a big deal," John Coyle said. "They got a really nice car to drive for the whole week." Coyle paused to make sure everyone was listening. "No kidding, ten straight weeks, Player of the Week—Chuck. Chuck gets three interceptions, Player of the Week—Chuck. Wink gets five touchdowns, Player of the Week—Chuck. Every week the coach makes a big deal about it." Coyle changed his voice to mimic Coach Miller. "Well, it was real close this week. But this game's Player of the Week—Chuck."

Everyone smiled at my father. It was clear Coach Miller had seen something in my father—a talent for the game that went beyond ability. But my father's skillful play didn't exempt him from Coach Miller's discipline.

"We're in Lucasville," my father said as we stood in Mary's kitchen. He was already laughing as he looked over at Mike Winkler. "Coach sends a player in with a play, and I decide to call a different play. I throw a long ball to Wink and Wink flies down the field. He beats his guy and catches the ball for a touchdown."

I looked back and forth between the two of them.

"Well, Coach calls me off and puts Danini in," my father said, holding onto his stomach through his laughter.

Winkler made a stern expression and gruffed his voice as he imitated Coach Miller.

"Coach said, 'That wasn't the play. Sit your butt down,'" Winkler said. He looked right at me as he imitated my father's innocent, exasperated response the day he disobeyed Coach Miller. "And then Chuck looked up at Coach and said, 'We just scored a touchdown, Coach!' And Coach looks over at Chuck and says, 'I didn't tell you to do that.'"

Winkler and my father both roared with laughter as everyone else watched them, smiling.

"Did you get Player of the Week?" I asked my father.

"No," my father said as tears rolled down his cheek. He nodded in Winkler's direction. "Wink got it."

The two of them laughed even harder.

"I smoked that guy," Winkler said as he slapped his hands together. It was obvious from the way Winkler smiled and the way my father shook his head laughing that it was Winkler's idea to call the renegade play against Lucasville.

When Winkler and I were alone in the kitchen, I asked him what it was really like to play against other schools in southern Ohio. Because they were a smaller school, they played schools in small, rural townships outside of Portsmouth proper. They were the only ones with an integrated roster. The memories they were all recalling seemed so pleasant, happy. Winkler seemed like the kind of guy who told the whole truth, perhaps unintentionally. I wanted to know about the stories my father wouldn't tell me or didn't remember.

"Portsmouth West was one of our biggest rivals," he said. "We had this statue of the Blessed Virgin Mary in the front of the school. They painted it black, you know, because of Al and your dad. They hated us."

Al Bass had gone to the Catholic middle school in Portsmouth like my father; they began attending Notre Dame High School in the fall of 1964—one year after the assassination of President John F. Kennedy.

Winkler placed his beer on the counter and held his hands in front of him as he told me more about Notre Dame's archrival, Portsmouth West High School—a school located in West Portsmouth, Ohio. It was a small school, like Notre Dame, but Portsmouth West filled their 20,000-seat stadium for every single home football game.

"They had this guy named Punky Wilson. He was killing us in this one game." Winkler leaned over into a three-point stance to re-enact the story—the fingertips of one hand pressed on Mary's kitchen floor, the other hand reaching behind and across his back, rear end in the air. "So during the game I lean over to Al on the line, and I say to him 'He just called you the "N" word.' And Al says, 'Which guy?' I point over at Punky Wilson and that was it. Al hits him on the next play. Knocks him over. 'Don't you ever call me the "N" word again!' Al works him over the rest of the game."

Winkler also remembered pulling up in front of Portsmouth West once for a game to find three local fire trucks parked out front near the football field. It hadn't rained in over a month, but the field was completely flooded.

"We were a fast team and they wanted to slow us down. But it didn't work," Winkler said.

Winkler told me that the mistreatment they experienced from students and fans at local schools didn't just occur during the football season. "We played some team in basketball—Manchester or Western Pike—some school way down on the river. They had never seen minorities in that area. They milked cows at halftime. They had the smallest gym in the world and Al and Chuck were the only black guys who had ever been there. After the game, those rednecks come out of nowhere. Next thing I know Al's laying on the ground. One of them clowns knocked him out."

I remember walking through a department store on the way back from lunch at the mall with my friends one day in high school. We were a large, unruly crowd of mostly boys and we were attracting attention as we meandered down the crowded aisles of Tupperware and toasters, voices boisterous. Two of my friends picked up toys at the end of the aisle and slipped them in their shirts non-discreetly as a dowdy clerk watched them. The clerk headed awkwardly towards us, glasses pushed up in frustration, her face matching her large, red employee golf shirt. The boys let the items drop from their shirts, laughing as they tossed the toys onto a shelf full of T-shirts. They almost knocked over a South Asian woman in traditional dress as they sauntered towards the doorway.

Someone told a "Paki" joke.

"You can't say that," I said. "What about Shaan?"

"I call Shaan a Paki to his face all the time," one guy responded.

They all laughed harder as we made our way through the department store exits. The cold, winter air made my face feel dry and papery. I slowed down and walked alone. I started to think about the kinds of jokes they told about people like me when I was not around to hear them—jokes about black people, women. I started to think how easy it was to be a young, white guy, particularly when you were athletic and handsome. I remember resentfully wiping away tears with my gruff wool mittens, hoping no one would notice.

At the homecoming football game, I asked Al Bass what he remembered about the games at Notre Dame High School.

"When we went to Portsmouth West, the parents had to escort us on the bus as soon as the game ended," Al said. "The fans threw stuff at us and tried to physically attack us. They did whatever they could. They punched us, used the 'N' word, all of it. We ran into that everywhere we played. Once we got out of Portsmouth proper and played some of those county schools, it was pretty tough." He stared down at the field as the opposing team intercepted a Notre Dame pass. "They did not like black athletes. They did not like blacks *period*," Al said.

Tom Danini nodded from his seat next to Al Bass—eyes on the field, head moving slowly from side to side. "Those were pretty groundbreaking times," Tom said.

On February 1, 1960, when my father was ten years old, four black students from North Carolina Agriculture and Technical

School entered a Woolworth's restaurant in downtown Greensboro, North Carolina, and sat at the lunch counter. Restaurant personnel instructed them to move to *their* section of the restaurant, in accordance with their policy of segregated dining areas. The four men ignored the demand. They remained in their seats at the counter without being served until the restaurant closed that evening. The next day they returned and sat at the lunch counter again without being served. NCAT students visited the diner every day and continued the peaceful protest for six months.

In July 1960, three local storeowners changed their policy to allow integrated counters that served people regardless of race or colour. The event marked the first sit-in of the civil rights movement, a time one writer would refer to as the "Negro Revolution," declaring it "the most important domestic event of the postwar period."

Two years after the sit-in in Greensboro—at a place in Portsmouth known as Dreamland—the issues of the civil rights movement would come to a head, because of a boy named Eugene McKinley.

Eugene McKinley presses his black face against the diamond-link fence outside Dreamland, Portsmouth's only swimming facility. He looks at the cool, blue water and wipes the sweat off his forehead, wishful. A sign that hangs near Eugene on the fence reads: *For card-holding members only.*

The summer sun covers the town in a hazy heat wave, and Eugene watches a boy in a red bucket hat, skin fair as dust, playing in the swimming pool. The boy's mother holds her son gently over the pale water; the little boy squeals and giggles. The toddler looks up through the fence at the black boy with the sweaty skin staring back at him. The little boy smiles and waves. The woman turns. When she sees Eugene, she places her son on her hip, his chubby legs gripped around her, and hurries towards the lifeguard. She points frantically in Eugene's direction, towards the fence with the sign on it. By the time the lifeguard makes his way over, Eugene is running down the road, back to Portsmouth's North End.

The next day, the heat wave continues, temperatures climbing steadily. Eugene and his friends decide to walk to the quarry—a small haven surrounded by messy coves and large rocks. Wild green leaves, vines, and large weeds stick out from the unpredictable landscape. There are no fences or membership cards or barriers for North End boys who are tired and swollen by the sun's rays. None of the boys know how to swim, but they all know how to soak. So they strip down and follow Eugene slowly, their feet on rocks and pressing into mud that squishes through their toes like oatmeal. They step down into the quarry and let the water's cool wrap around them.

Murky liquid slips between their ankles and knees, and they close their eyes in relief, cool pulsing through their veins, mouths gaping satisfaction. They splash and toss handfuls of water on their faces, rub the warm wetness down their arms, let it drip between their fingers.

Eugene wades deeper, away from the boys, the water creeping upwards—waist, belly, chest, further. He holds his arms up, then leans back and lets the water lift him to the surface. His toes peek out, the back of his head, his ears, underwater. He waves his arms like wings, back then forward. Suddenly. A pull. He gasps. His head snaps upright, his feet in search of footing but finding nothing. He slaps his arms against the water, then he goes under.

The boys shout out at him. "Eugene!"

He paddles up, head surfacing. Another pull.

"*Heee—bblblbbl!*"

Eugene's fingers scrape the surface, but something sucks him downward. He swings his arms, kicks his legs frantically, his mouth open, his eyes wide with fear, surrounded by bubbles of water. The boys call again, and again, but Eugene continues to wrestle and the boys see only concentric rings that dissipate on the surface. They step out of the water in fright, stand on the shore and watch the water wave, spread, then slow to nothing.

"Eugene was my cousin," my father said when Tom brought up the event that took place at Dreamland the summer after Eugene's drowning, while we were standing in Mary Barry's kitchen.

"It was a private pool," Tom explained.

"The pool was segregated," my father corrected. "And we had a sit-in. I was thirteen."

"They dropped their money down and hopped over the gate," Tom said.

"Well, three or four of them did that," my father said. "Roy Bates and some of the other guys. They dropped their money down, jumped over the gate, and ran towards the pool. The rest of us sat out front."

"Because they were in the pool, the lifeguard yelled, 'Clear the pool,'" Tom remembered. "We were sitting nearby playing cards." Tom turned to my father pensively. "I looked through the fence and I saw you. I remember saying, 'There's Chuck.'"

"I was being taken away from the pool in a paddy wagon," my father explained to me.

At the homecoming football game, Tom Danini looked out onto the field.

"We were all there in the pool as card-holding members and Chuck was outside."

Tom had lived in Los Angeles and Canada after leaving Portsmouth to go to school; his Italian skin was as brown as mine that summer. I looked at him for a while, in profile, his eyes glazed. I could tell this was hard for him to think about, to remember. He was watching that sit-in happen all over again.

"We all grew up together. We were playing together since sixth grade. We lived within blocks of each other."

He shook his head as the cheerleaders rallied the crowd. A group of identically clad white girls in the gold and blue of Notre Dame High School stretched out signs that read: *Hold that line.*

"Some of the parents were warm and accepted the guys," he said. "But then on the other side of that, you would hear racial terms and undertones. I got dual messages from my parents. It was really confusing."

Tom lived on the other side of the tracks, at the top of a hill that separated my father and his two black classmates from their white peers. Tom remembered watching my father, Al, and Gerald Underwood head down to the North End on their way home from school. He remembered swimming whenever he was hot. He remembered watching my father get loaded into a paddy wagon, and seeing my father's face peering back at him from the blackness behind the bars as the rest of his classmates from Notre Dame returned to their card game.

It was hard for me to imagine my father sitting with his back pressed against that fence line, riding in a paddy wagon. My father didn't seem to protest much of anything.

"Did you encounter racism when you were younger?" I heard a young man ask him at a speaking engagement in Portsmouth.

"Well, yes, sort of," he said. "I mean, it was the sixties."

Then he moved on to the next question. My father presented those times with mild disdain, mediocre disapproval. It was something we disagreed about—something that stemmed from a significant difference between the two of us.

When it came to our emotions, my father expressed a range of mild subtleties. His anger was similar in execution to his expressions of elation, while I had a range of mountain-high and valley-low reactions. I could manoeuvre from ecstatic excitement to utter dismay speedily and easily, based on what I deemed necessary. Which meant that throughout my adolescence my father and I rarely experienced the same event with the same level of expression. It's why I was frustrated by his recall of the times, of his diminished account of the difficulties of the civil rights movement. There was a lot that I was missing.

Two hours before my high school prom in 1999, the hotel we were going to for an after party notified us that they were terminating all of my classmates' reservations. I was head of the Prom Committee, which meant I had planned and coordinated all the events, and secured limousines for them. The hotel was now saying teenagers were wild, rowdy, messy, and unreliable; they had cancelled the reservations of everyone connected with my high school.

My parents hadn't wanted me to do a hotel after party. We were a conservative, Christian family. I shouldn't be hanging out at hotels overnight when there were boys there. My mother was being supportive, but inside I believed she was secretly elated by the divinely orchestrated intervention meant to save me from temptation and godlessness.

When my father came home from work, I was crying in my prom dress. My mother explained what had happened. I expected him to shrug, to point out the relative insignificance of the unfortunate mishap in the grand scheme of important happenings. But without changing his suit or removing his tie, without conferring with my mother over what should be done, my father got on the phone and asked to speak with the manager at the hotel where we had made our reservation. He told them that he wouldn't do any more business there if this was how they treated their customers. If his credit card wasn't good enough now, it wouldn't be later. I was dumbfounded.

My father shied away from conversations with me when I was a teenager. The conversations we did have were minimal and limited in word count. They were filled with dramatic pauses, rolled eyes, and huffing on both of our parts. We had already avoided discussions about the prom, because our views were so different. My father thought the whole thing was excessive. When four hundred engraved champagne flutes arrived at our house in large boxes and when hundreds of fancy black invitation cards were stuffed into envelopes by classmates gathered after school in our family room, my father added to his silent disapproval by nodding with a quick, disappearing smile as a fear-filled group of teens stared up at him.

When I heard about the sit-in at Dreamland during Mary Barry's party, and when I discussed it again with Tom Danini at the football game, I wondered if I was wrong to interpret my father's actions as passive. I thought of the decisive way he handled my prom after-party fiasco. Maybe there was another way of doing things, of handling challenges. Perhaps my father's quiet grace could help me address the confusion I felt about the depth and measure of my blackness.

6

I GREW UP in a three-bedroom, detached house in Mississauga with my father, mother, sister and brother. My mother was in charge of everything house- and children-related. She cooked and cleaned and organized our schedules while my father worked to afford this mutually agreed-on arrangement. She was there every day when I got home from school and came to every game, every recital, and every theatre performance. I never heard my parents speak about a shortage of money. Although my mother often lamented the dishes she was left to clean up, and although my father was away too often, we were happy.

By the time I got married and moved into a basement apartment with my husband, we were each working two jobs. I realized how hard it was going to be to afford the kind of life I'd had throughout my childhood. And when I saw the North End where my father grew up, where his own father had walked away and left him with nothing, I realized that in one generation, my father had changed everythiing.

"This is the North End," my father said as we bumped our way over the railroad tracks.

There were small, bungalows facing the main road. A few were neat and well cared for. Most of them were forlorn and neglected. There were old brick churches, and a series of houses adjacent to them that had been converted to places of worship.

My father pulled into a townhouse complex. We got out of the car, and I breathed in the smell of summer heat and black concrete. Damon and I looked at one another—he with Asher in his arms, me with a baby four months along in my belly. We were thinking the same thing and we said just as much later when my father was walking ahead of us: This is where we came from.

We followed my father down a sidewalk flanked with low, green bushes. Tall lamps lined the walkway and curved over top of us. My father stopped in front of one of the townhouse units.

"This is where I used to live. My grandmother and I would watch for my mother to come home from work from that very window."

The house was part of a row of ten units that faced a similar row on the opposite side of the walkway. There was a wooden roof over the front door that was painted a dull, murky brown, which contrasted with the yellow brick. There was one rectangular window on the first floor, and another large one that looked out from the second storey.

"I used to watch for my mother coming home from work from that very window with my grandmother," my father told us.

A young white boy walked out of the house, headphones plugged into his ears, glasses up over his eyes, as though he didn't notice us. I watched him until he walked all the way out of the complex. I wanted to say something. I wanted to know if there were signs of my father's childhood, memories left somewhere inside the house where he grew up. I wanted to see if his name was etched on the walls or on the floorboards; I wanted to see if his growth was marked with scratch marks on the doorframes.

My father often appears quiet and serious. But when he tells stories about life in the North End—the positive stories where life is about the community and the friendships he had, not the financial struggles or his father's absence—his face is bright, his eyes windows to a life of misadventures. It was this side of my father that I started to see as we walked away from his old townhouse towards the local baseball diamond. My father leaned on the post of the grey link fence, and I looked around at the park as I stood next to him. I recognized the spot from old video footage I had seen, where lean boys leaped across makeshift hurdles in jeans and white T-shirts.

"Do you want to know how I learned to run?" my father said, smile stretching mischievously.

I nodded. I wanted to know everything.

"Larry and Lee were the big guys and they used to play a game of chase at night. They would chase us through the projects, past clotheslines and garbage cans. If they caught you, they got to pound your legs and give you a charley horse. It was like tag. The big guys chased the little guys. That's how I learned to run."

His smile deepened and he started to laugh as I stared at him, my eyebrows curved in confusion.

I had a charley horse once in my right calf. It felt like my lower leg was cinched in a vise—a tight squeeze inside my calf that made my blood rush and pulse, inside a small cramped space painfully. Only my father was smiling as he remembered the charley horses from his childhood.

We walked around the baseball diamond, along a grassy patch shadowed by a stretch of small trees. When we reached a sewer drain, my father stopped and started to laugh. He began to tell me about the other games he played during his childhood.

June Bug Kites: Catch a June bug. Tie the June bug's legs with a piece of long string and let it fly around in circles. See whose bug is the fastest. My father made a buzzing sound, his finger moving towards my ear like a June bug captive on a string. I swatted him away and frowned. He let out a loud, exuberant cackle.

Bean Shooter Wars: Go to Mrs. Ramsey's and purchase a nickel's worth of pinto beans. Build a shooter from found materials. Form it carefully and decorate it for the purposes of identification and maximum trajectory. Shoot the pinto beans at your opponent like machine guns.

"Stevie Battle could hit you with a bean shooter once and just knock you over," my father said, his head shaking as he smiled, teeth bared, still impressed by Stevie's bean shooter abilities. Stevie Battle is Kathleen Battle's brother. His sister is Portsmouth's internationally renowned opera singer. There must be something in the lungs of those Battle kids.

Popsicle Stick Races (A Rainy Day Activity): Take a Popsicle stick and place it in street water. The first Popsicle stick to slide into the sewer wins. I looked at the sewer drain embedded in the curb, then stared at my father incredulously.

"What else were we supposed to do when it rained?" he said.

I asked my mother if she played similar games and my father laughed boisterously. "Your mother was rich."

"I played hopscotch and I skipped," my mother said, shrugging awkwardly, as though ashamed or uncomfortable. "I rode my bike like the other kids in the neighbourhood."

The games my father had described to me were not just games played by the North End boys. They were the games of poor, black kids in the sixties. Popsicle sticks and beans and string were much more affordable than jump ropes and bicycles.

My mother was born in Chicago and grew up in Toledo on the nice side of town to parents who both had university degrees and full-time jobs—a principal and a social worker. She was the latchkey kid of two highly educated black professionals long before those kinds of credentials were normal in black families. With her unique upbringing, my mother had something in common with her children, something that set us apart from my father—none of us had any first-hand knowledge of black poverty.

"The problem with living in Portsmouth at the time was that I didn't know anything else," my father told me later. "So I didn't have a whole bunch of things to compare it to. The only thing I knew was it was a small town. I had a pretty good living. It wasn't that bad other than being what most people considered poor."

When we got back in the car, my father took us by an old building in the North End with boarded-up windows that were covered in graffiti. It was the Fourteenth Street Community Center, where my father had spent much of his childhood.

My grandmother had arrived in Portsmouth just around the time the Fourteenth Street Community Center was erected, across from the Farley Street Housing Project. The Board of Directors, which was made up of representatives from all of the black churches in town, eventually deeded the property and the building to the city in exchange for water, sewers, electricity, and maintenance. The Center served as a social, recreational, and educational hub for Portsmouth's black community.

There was a place called the Dam on the second floor of the mall near my high school that I went to during lunch with some of my friends when the security guards kicked us out of the food court. It was a space that had housed a department store, but was now rented by a community group that worked to help teens in rough times. There were card tables, computers, pool tables, and a room where you could graffiti anything that came to mind on blank, white wall space: I luv Backstreet Boys; School Sucks; Girls Rule. There were field trips and after-school drop-in programs for kids who had parents but rarely saw them; there were programs in the evenings and on weekends for kids who were homeless. Standing by at all hours of the day were counsellors waiting to help kids who were looking for a way out of their circumstances—teen girls who'd gotten pregnant, heavy drug users, kids full of promise who felt restricted by seemingly impossible obstacles. The staff at the Dam wanted to help troubled youth stay in Mississauga, a suburban environment that was safe and familiar in comparison with downtown Toronto, where statistics showed they would succumb to greater hardship and tragedy.

During lunch hours, I would read the advertisements for their programs while I played solitaire on the computers. When counsellors tried to strike up casual conversations, I tried to imply with my demeanour that I was not like those other kids they worked with. I was not at-risk or in trouble. I often wondered if I knew of anyone who needed the help they were offering.

On Friday nights, the Fourteenth Street Community Center held a dance for teens in the North End. In January 1963, my father turned thirteen and attended his first of many dances there. Before the dance he and his friends shared a bottle of Thunderbird wine, which an older boy had purchased for them from the corner store.

"Thunderbird's the word," my father said as he remembered the old slogan. He stared at the abandoned building in front of us. "If you were dancing too closely during a slow song, they would flip on the lights. Everyone would split up," he said with a mischievous grin. "You weren't allowed to dance like that."

"South of Toledo, slow dancing meant grinding," my mother added.

I thought about my wedding—my siblings' weddings—how my father walked onto the dance floor in his black tuxedo and shiny shoes, how he stepped and swaggered, rotated in repetition around the floor doing the electric slide to the sounds of Michael Jackson. Your dad is smooth, my friends said when they saw that side of him.

I looked at the old building that was once the Fourteenth Street Community Center. This was where he learned to move.

"I used to go back to the Center when I came home for a visit," my father said. "They had this board there—they posted notes about what people were up to, who had died. It's how we stayed connected."

In 2002, the City of Portsmouth's Engineering Department declared the original Fourteenth Street Community Center structurally unsafe and closed the facility. Programs were operating temporarily out of church basements and the 17th Street Armoury when I was there in 2008. The old notes about the community, about the people who the Center serviced, no longer existed. Drugs and delinquency were ravaging the neighbourhood.

I looked at the empty building that had once been the heart of the neighbourhood—the place where young people had their first dance, and snuck their first drink and their first kisses. I wish I had come to Portsmouth earlier.

"How did Grandma and your father meet?" I asked my father soon after we returned to Canada, on an autumn day when the leaves were falling on the grass in drops of orange and yellow.

My father pressed mute on the TV remote control and shrugged. "Probably at the Supper Club."

The Supper Club was where black residents in Portsmouth spent their nights out. Although it was no longer in operation when I visited there in 2008, it's likely that my grandmother and Chuck Senior met there before my grandfather left for the war.

In the early sixties, after Chuck Senior and my grandmother were officially divorced, it was a man named George Spaulding who would garner my grandmother's attention. My father referred to him as Uncle George.

"What about Uncle George?" I said. "How did they meet?"

"Same. That's where everyone in the North End met. There was a lot of that going on. Especially after the war," my father said. "You just knew that this guy, who was once with this other lady, was now living in your home."

"Did Grandpa and Uncle George know each other?"

My father shrugged. "Probably."

I knew less about Uncle George than I did about my grand-father, despite the fact that he had lived with my father for a significant part of his childhood. I wondered if he was tall, big, or handsome. I concluded he was all three—the first two because my father said he worked on the railroad and that he was a soldier; the last because when I imagined a man my grandmother loved, I imagined one I would love too. Only when I asked my father what Uncle George was like, he shook his head and frowned. He said he couldn't remember.

"Was he abusive?"

My father shifted on the couch. "She hit him, he hit her. But it was only when they drank."

My father stared at the TV in pensive silence as I imagined my grandmother at the Supper Club with Uncle George, music moving them slow and smooth around the dance floor.

The couple presses closer together, my grandmother's cheek against George's broad shoulder, his thick arms hold-ing her as they swirl around the floor to jazzy blues. A man stumbles towards them, breath and sweat thick with liquor.

"Earline, I need-ta talk wid you," the man says, slow, careful, but slurring.

George lets go of his partner and steps back stiffly. My grandmother steadies the man as he heads towards the bar and waves at the bartender. The bartender grabs a glass and pours a drink, eyeing the man cautiously.

"What do you want, Charles?" my grandmother finally asks him.

"I need—" Chuck Senior blinks and when his eyes open wide again, cloudy and yellowed, he says just what she expected. She dips her hand into her clutch purse and slides a few bills discreetly under his glass and another towards the bartender.

On the way home, my grandmother wraps her arm around George's full biceps, squeezing him against her. The heels of her shoes click-click against the concrete.

"I don't want you talkin' ta Charles," George says, pulling his arm back.

She shoves George gently, voice crooning through the sultry night. "Geoooorge."

He waves her away and keeps walking, space between them. "I don't want you talkin' ta him, Earline. I mean it."

"He was asking about Junior," she says as her heels click faster to keep up with him.

"You think I'm stupid?" he says.

George makes his way up the short path to the house and leans against the doorframe. My grandmother unlocks the door and steps inside. He follows, stumbling slightly.

"That man don't care about Junior. He just wants all he can git from you."

She whispers, "Please, George. Junior might hear you."

He flips his hand and laughs, then says even louder, "Trust me. He done figured out by now his daddy don't care 'bout him."

"His daddy cares just fine," she mutters, as she places her purse on the table.

Although when George grabs her throat and presses her head against the wall—five thick fingers around the flesh of her neck, his wide hand pushed against her jawbone—she wonders why she said this, why she's defending her ex-husband.

"Is he here paying your bills?" George says through teeth that are gritted and rotten.

She tries to move but George squeezes tighter and when she tries to exhale the strain makes her eyes fill up with water.

"Please," she whispers, full of panic.

"Junior?" George yells, grinning wickedly.

The house is still and quiet, and my grandmother prays for air, because it's disappearing.

"He's out," George says into her ear with a hot, breathy whisper. "Just like his daddy."

My grandmother strikes George's arm, then his face, her eyes wild and frantic, her face in red distress, her body failing. He squeezes his fingers deeper into her neck, as the room turns grey and smoky, flooding with blackness. A light comes on suddenly, and George releases his hold. My grandmother gasps and blinks, sliding to the floor. Near the light switch, a young man stares stern and steady.

———————————

"There were a lot of things that felt like they were just a part of life back then. I didn't like some of the moments but I would wake up and it was all over," my father told me. "I didn't know anything else. Most of the men were abusive back then. My focus was on not getting too caught up in it other than to make sure my mother was okay."

While George and my grandmother never married, and while my grandmother suffered multiple miscarriages, eventually she and George had a child together. When my father was fifteen, my grandmother gave birth to a boy they named Bryant Spaulding.

When my father told me about his brother and the troubles he had with George Spaulding, I asked him how he knew about the miscarriages. Had his mother spoken to him about them? Did he hear her crying in the bathroom?

"I just sort of gathered from the way things were that something had happened," my father told me.

I nodded because I had learned a lot of things about my father that way already—through observation, inferences, and his perplexing silences. To cope with the difficulties of the sixties, my father chose to rely not on alcohol or violence or drugs, but on something altogether different. It was how my father would ensure that his story turned out far differently than those of Chuck Senior and George Spaulding.

7

M Y FATHER WAS SCHEDULED to take part in a homecoming parade on the second day of our visit to
Portsmouth. Homecoming festivities are popular
in American cities. They are one of my favourite American
traditions—a weekend of celebrations that include an annual
parade, tailgating events, and a football game. Townspeople
would celebrate the place they currently live or formerly resided
in under an umbrella of marching band music, balloons, and
confetti. I admire the way Americans celebrate community
and a common history.

For most people in southwestern Ontario, "home" means
elsewhere: the Caribbean, India, Italy, Portugal, China, Pakistan. We celebrate our international culture more than our current places of Canadian residence. It's why it's sometimes hard to
distinguish what it means to be Canadian.

It has always been hard for me to clearly identify the differences between where my father was raised and where I was
born—to have a right perspective on black culture and American history. Homecoming weekend seemed like the ideal place
for clarification. I wanted to get a better understanding on the
town and the community that raised my father and inevitably
shaped our family.

The starting point—and marshalling grounds—for the home-coming parade in Portsmouth was a parking lot that stretched across the front of two large structures. One was a high, oval stone wall that was weathered in shades of grey. The other was a baseball stadium. The two were separated by a narrow section of the parking lot; along the back end of this area, a tall grassy hill rose high over top of them.

We parked next to the stone wall as the afternoon sun rose mercilessly above us. Cars, tractors, and floats from local high schools and organizations were lining up in a long row that snaked through the parking lot. There were old-fashioned cars, tractors, men on horseback, themed floats with jungle scenes, and fire stations made out of cardboard, papier mâché, and tissue paper.

My father led us on foot down the narrow lot between the stone wall and the baseball stadium. Near the back of the long line of paraders, we found my father's parade car behind Notre Dame's Greek mythology–themed float. A group of young girls and a boy with a giant feather fan on a long pole gathered in togas. My father's name was printed in bold capitals on signs that were hanging off both sides of the vehicle.

Coordinators for the parade came to the car, clipboards clutched to their chests. They gave my father some instructions and advised us to stay put and wait. The parade will be starting soon, they told us. When they turned away, camp-style caps shielding their periphery, my father checked his watch and waved for us to follow him. We walked, past little girls with tight blond curls who cartwheeled and flipped in pleated costumes, until the last of the floats were behind us and the grassy hill stood high in front of us. My father gestured us upwards.

Damon and Asher climbed up first, my brother's strong steps matched by the speed of his son's quick motion. My mother followed. The hill wasn't high, but at the start of my second trimester, my balance had begun to falter. My first step slipped, and I gripped my belly instinctively. I placed my foot cautiously in a more distinct groove of dirt as my father extended his hand towards me. I smiled and slid my hand onto his; he continued to steady me upwards. I noted for the first time how the change inside me had also changed my father. He was sensitive to what I needed and instinctively supportive. He understood that I was fragile.

At the top of the hill, long grass tickled up to our knees. Down below, a wide river rushed by, lined with trees whose limbs bent and curved towards the water, sipping small waves that flowed along the surface. Further down the river, a white bridge crossed towards what looked like the side of a small mountain, green with foliage.

"That's the Ohio River. And that's Kentucky," my father said, pointing.

Four-year-old Asher tapped his grandfather's knee. "Where, Poppa? I can't see Kin-tucky."

My father grabbed his grandson under his arms, lifted him in the air, and placed him on his shoulder. He pointed again at the green landscape on the other side of the river.

I stood there with my father and brother, my mother and my nephew, as sweat dripped down my spine. I thought about how the banks below had served as shelter, the river an overwhelming obstacle, and the sun a hopeful guide for slaves who were headed north more than a century earlier, under the pursuit of slave hunters and hungry bloodhounds. I wondered where home was for them—the place where they came from or the place they were hoping to get to.

I listened to the water rush for a moment, then looked back down on the parking lot where floats and people moved like bees on a honeycomb. From where we stood, I could see inside the massive oval, framed with a wall of beige brick and mortar.

There were rows of bleachers that curved around the stadium, grass striped in neat, white lines, uprights at either end of it. I turned to my father, filled with excitement.

"Is that the wall from the story?"

My father looked down at the stadium and then smiled at me.

A group of boys peer over their shoulders, careful and cautious, as the sky slowly darkens. They hover in the shadows, near the walls of Municipal Stadium as the sound of the Ohio River rushes in the background. They listen for the sound of police officers and fans rising to their feet, their hats pressed to their chest, standing at full attention. They wait for the music.

Oh say can you see. Hands placed on the cool of the wall, fingers gripped tightly, the boys start upwards. Feet in the grooves, they climb higher. *By the dawn's early light.* Their bodies pressed against the stone, their knees, feet, ankles gripping rock-wall. *What so proudly we hailed.* The police officers inside and outside the stadium stand completely still, hands angled sharply across stern brows. *At the twilight's last gleaming.* The boys climb higher, legs pushing upward. *Whose broad stripes and bright stars.* Their breath breaking unevenly. *Through the perilous fight.* Sweat beads on their foreheads. *O'er the ramparts we watched.* Until their hands finally feel the flatness at the top of their obstacle. *Were so gallantly streaming.* They push once more and swing their legs over, sitting upright. *And the rocket's red glare.* Pause. *The bombs bursting in air.* They look down at the packed stadium. *Gave proof through the night.* Under the lights, the stars and stripes waving. *That our flag was still there.* They smile at the view. *Does that star-spangled banner yet wave?* They step down into the stands in waves of black bodies. *O'er the land of the free.* Scatter themselves among football foes and fans discreetly. *And the home of the brave.* They watch the entire football game before making their way back down the hill, across the North End train tracks.

"The police got smarter though," my father told me. "They started to spread molasses all over the top of the wall. But that didn't stop us. We just brought newspapers and placed them on our stomachs and on the top of the wall so we wouldn't get stuck."

I watched my father carefully as we stood on that hill looking down at the walls of Municipal Stadium. I had never thought of him as adventurous before, never known him as a risk taker. On vacations he found a routine and stuck with it—golf, pool, dinner. Nothing wild, risky, or out of the ordinary. I tried to imagine him younger, a stone wall scaler. Standing on that hill, looking at Municipal Stadium with him reinforced that my father was more than the person from my childhood.

In a homecoming parade where my father was once honoured as Grand Marshall, I sat on a green lawn covered with autumn leaves and waited for my father to appear between the hordes of cartwheeling clowns, drumming bands, and sequinned dancers with sparkling batons. Skye, Damon, and I, and all of my nephews wore shirts with my father's name and number on them. We watched my mother and father roll down the street towards us, then disappear down another road, waving like the royal family.

My brother and I planned to do the same in Portsmouth—find a patch of grass, where we would wait, watch, and wave as he and my mother rode past us. But when my father's scheduled driver at the Portsmouth homecoming parade offered up his role, my father asked my brother to drive the convertible. I hopped in the passenger seat. Asher was placed on the back seat between my father and my mother.

When all of the floats and cars were lined up and ready, the parade volunteers motioned the caravan forward. Damon drove the car slowly behind Notre Dame's Greek float, as the parade moved onto the cracked, grey streets of Portsmouth. When the caravan curled left, the girls stumbled, hands gripping cotton sheet togas and pressing down against the olive branches that were sliding down their foreheads; a young blonde in red stirrup pants and rubber boots on the fire station float behind us held onto her papier mâché brick wall to keep it from falling.

A crowd lined the road a few feet back from the floats on the first street we drove down. Some were seated on the curb or on the beds of pickup trucks; some were standing at the end of their driveway. Others rocked back and forth on chairs and benches that creaked loudly from their porches. As our car passed the onlookers, serious faces smiled, fingers pointed. I thought it was the girls in the togas, or the blonde faux-firefighter. But the grey-haired men in faded denim standing next to American pick-up trucks were smiling at my father.

"That's Chuck Ealey. Best quarterback in college football. Went to Notre Dame," said one gentleman. I pretended not to notice the indifferent expression of the young man whose dark hair was pressed wet against his forehead, underneath his ball cap. He simply nodded and looked right at me, not my father, as our car rolled past him.

The houses along the parade route were beautifully old. They had wood siding and wraparound front porches, good-sized lawns, and lengthy driveways. Some houses had flowers in bloom, American flags resting flatly in the heavy heat of summer, but many of the houses were dilapidated and failing—flags tattered and torn, sections of siding missing, lawns overwhelmed with weeds, roofs sunken. On one house, the roof was riddled with so many gaping holes I wondered how anyone could live in it. I wondered how they managed when it rained or how they made it through the winter.

As we turned down another street, wide women sat a few feet away in lawn chairs that scooped low to the ground; they held ice cream cones and hot dogs from a nearby snack stand as barefoot children slipped between the floats in search of candy. Only we didn't have any, and I remember those children staring up at me blankly.

I spotted a little girl with a white-blond bob that curled under her chin when the caravan of floats stopped for a moment. She was nearly two and the bottoms of her feet were black from walking barefoot on the asphalt. I watched her waddle across the road wearing a large, white T-shirt with dirty brown handprints, her grey diaper drooping low between her knees. She looked at me with turquoise eyes and I waved, but she didn't smile or wave back at me.

We drove into downtown Portsmouth, past old rundown shops, empty stores, an orange multi-storey building with brown metal rails where residents leaned on balconies. People watched and waved at us, bottles in hand, cigarettes dangling off their lips precariously. I tried to keep looking forward. Underneath my glasses, I could feel the burn of tears threatening.

In 2007, the average income in Portsmouth hovered at around $25,000 per year, barely over 50 per cent of the state average. About a quarter of the people in Portsmouth lived below the poverty line. At the time of our visit, America was headed towards a detrimental recession. Towns like Portsmouth would suffer the worst of the fallout. They had already started to experience the economic downturn, and the atmosphere felt weighted under their financial challenges.

The rural areas of Ontario, my own rural-town university neighbourhood, were different from what I saw in Portsmouth that weekend. In Canada small towns feel quaint, cozy—branches of corporate banks housed in old homes with gates and freshly painted fences and shutters, flower baskets hanging from the metal branches of old, black lampposts.

Portsmouth was my father's hometown, but it felt foreign and unfamiliar. When I saw the houses and the people along the parade route, I was gripped by their struggle. I wanted to get out of the car, to go back home, to forget what I saw there. Without my father I would have been right there with them—abandoned and forgotten between foothills and the banks of the Ohio River, by a country struggling to save itself.

8

I SPENT a long time thinking about what I saw in Portsmouth when I was back in Canada—about poverty and privilege, about the differences between black and white people on both sides of the border. I thought about how definitive those dichotomies were in America, and how much less so they were in Canada, where black and white, poor and privileged lived in mixed neighbourhoods, in proximity.

Throughout my adolescence the thoughts and beliefs I had about what it meant to be black, in particular, significantly impacted my relationships. It changed my relationship with Lorraine West and it influenced the decisions I made about dating; it forced me to consider not only what I looked like, but also how I saw myself and the world as a black woman.

When I learned about Portsmouth and Notre Dame, it made me wonder how my father handled issues of race in high school back in the sixties.

In 1958, six years before my father started to attend Notre Dame High School, a black woman named Mildred Delores Jeter and a white man named Richard Perry Loving fell in love. They lived in the state of Virginia, but travelled to nearby Washington D.C., where interracial marriages were legal.

When Mildred and Richard returned home from their wedding, a group of police officers—likely tipped off by neighbours or watchdog authorities—invaded their home hoping to find the couple consummating their marriage (a state offence that carried a more severe penalty than their marriage did). Although unsuccessful in that goal, law enforcement discovered the couple's marriage certificate hanging on the wall of their bedroom. The Lovings were consequently arrested.

On January 6, 1959, my father's ninth birthday, the Lovings pleaded guilty and were sentenced to one year in prison. The judge agreed to suspend their sentence on one condition: the couple would have to leave their home and the state of Virginia—where both of their families resided. They could not return together, or at the same time, or they would be arrested.

"Almighty God created the races white, black, yellow, malay, and red," the judge said, "and he placed them on separate continents. And but for the interference with this arrangement there would be no cause for such marriages . . . He did not intend for the races to mix."

In 1967, the United States Supreme Court finally ruled that prohibiting interracial marriage was unconstitutional. Virginia and the other fifteen states that still banned interracial marriage were forced to revise their laws. Mildred and Richard Loving were legally able to return to their hometown and visit their families together as a couple for the first time in nearly ten years.

That same year, my father attended a mixed community dance with a friend he referred to as James "Lemon" Luscious. I asked my father why he called James "Lemon."

"He was 'high yella,'" my father said with a smile. James had fair skin—butterscotch brown-yellow, like mine.

At some point during the social, James and my father invited two white girls to take a drive—Sarah Hastings and a friend whose name my father couldn't remember. Sarah sat in the front seat next to my father, James and the other girl in the back. My father drove the car to a quiet spot under a bridge near the railroad station just outside the North End.

My father puts the car in park, crickets creaking in the distance, dragonflies hovering. The foursome talks about school or the civil rights movement as Diana Ross reflects on the way life used to be on the radio. A car pulls up behind them. Round headlights flood bright light through the back window, shining intermittent blinks of red and blue colour. Sarah turns back, then quickly forward. James looks at his friend in the rear-view mirror, but my father's eyes are fixed on the figure walking towards them. The man is slow, careful, his footsteps direct and deliberate, his boot soles crunching on the stones that pave the shoulder. Crick. Crick. Crick.

Sarah and my father look at one another. He nods assurance that doesn't resonate, then turns off the radio. The steps get closer, until thick white fingers grip the driver's door, the window buried inside of it. A police officer leans in, flashlight beaming back and forth between the two rows.

"Evening, Officer," Lemon says cordially, leaning forward, palms up, showing both hands are empty.

"Everything okay tonight?" the officer says.

"Yes, Officer," my father says and the officer points his light directly at my father. My father lifts his hand over his eyes to make a shadow.

"That you, Chuck?"

"Yes, sir," my father says. Officer Hermann Smith was an insurance agent before he became a police officer. My grandmother was one of his clients.

"What you doing out here? Party's back in town."

"We just went for a little drive, sir."

"Don't look like you all's doin' much drivin' to me."

"We're just talking, Officer," the girl in the back says, voice tinged with anger. Sarah turns and glares at her.

My father keeps his hands on the wheel as Hermann Smith points the light towards the back and leans further into the vehicle. Sarah turns away, shielding her face, wishing her friend would just stay quiet.

"Your parents know you're out with these boys?" Smith says.

The girl rolls her eyes, arms crossed over her chest. The officer turns the flashlight on Sarah who's shaking all over.

"What 'bout you? Come on, stop hiding, young lady."

Sarah lowers her hands and squints into the flashlight.

"Miss Hastings?" he says.

She smiles weakly. Officer Smith steps back, flashlight on my father's profile.

"You girls go home right now, ya hear?"

My father nods, starts the car, but the two girls don't say anything.

"Ya'll hear me?" the officer says again.

"Yes, sir."

Back at the dance, the two girls separate from my father and James Luscious. Twenty minutes later, Brian Hastings, lawyer for the Portsmouth Police and Member of the Board at Portsmouth High, barges into the function having been pulled out of the movie theatre by police officers who told him about the incident. My father watches from a distance as Mr. Hastings takes his daughter by the arm and loads her into his vehicle.

While my father claimed that there was nothing going on between him and Sarah at the time, and while he downplayed the impact of the incident, Sarah Hastings's family took what happened that night very seriously.

"I was told I destroyed the family," Sarah told me when we spoke over the phone recently.

Sarah was threatened by girls at Portsmouth High School and harassed about that night, after police officers told scandalous lies that spread like hungry wildfire. Her father never believed her side of the story, and prohibited her from seeing or contacting my father.

"I have never gotten over it," she told me.

My father just shook his head when I told him about my conversation with Sarah.

"We weren't even doing anything," he told me.

"How were you treated at Notre Dame?" I asked my father, following our trip to Portsmouth.

My father looked puzzled, and answered quickly. "I was treated fine."

"So, you could date your classmates?"

"Well, no," he said. "It was the sixties."

This is where our conversations typically ended—my father confused by my approach, me irritated with his contradictory responses. But I needed clarity.

"So, for school dances and homecoming, did you go alone?"

"We were allowed to bring our own dates—Gerald, Al, and me."

"Could your classmates bring a date?"

"Everyone else had to bring dates from school. But we could bring our own."

He made it sound like it was a privilege. I wondered if he was doing that for me, or if that's how he wanted to remember it. I waited. There was something he wanted to tell me. He took off his glasses and laid them on the table.

"Our junior year, we had a dance," he said. "Gerald decided he wanted to dance with a friend, one of our classmates. He asked the girl to dance and she agreed." My father shook his head. "In the middle of the song, people started walking off the dance floor. It's the seniors that started it, the class above us. They all just walked off the dance floor and the juniors followed. The song ended and that's pretty much it."

"What did you do?"

He shrugged. "The next day, I asked my classmates what that was about. They said they didn't really know what was going on. The seniors just told them to get off the dance floor and they did. They didn't know what was happening or why they were doing it. I told them not to do something like that again. I told them it was just stupid."

The black and white issues that I faced when I was in high school were different from my father's. The division was still there, but instead of being forced to befriend and date people who looked like me, I could choose the people I associated with. Crossovers were rare—most people choosing to stay with those of similar background or appearance.

In Canada, I was perceived as being mixed or having a significant genetic whiteness, because my skin was fair and my hair curled in long, soft spirals. It made the crossover to a white group of friends easier. White was somewhere in my blood, after all, according to everyone who saw me. Only my decision to have white friends instead of black ones was confusing. It meant that I spent much of my adolescence pretending to be someone other people could accept. I became a kind of social chameleon— aware of what was needed to blend into each environment, and willing to quickly change in order to do so. It meant I spent very little time considering what I actually liked and wanted.

Being black meant sitting at the First Table exclusively. So at the First Table, I talked about hip-hop and R&B, reggae, and jazz music. No rock and no country. I tried to use words of exclamation like *sick*, *phat*, *fly*, and *dope*, in smooth and natural ways. I only talked about black guys. Being black meant spending weekends with Lorraine at gospel concerts or black people barbecues. If I ventured outside this environment, if I was spotted doing something with white people, I got called names connected with being white, "stush," or stuck-up. The most common name was Oreo, because the cookie has a chocolate-brown exterior and a sugary white filling. It meant I was only black on the outside.

In the white world, I watched hockey and followed baseball. I followed Canadian rock bands like the Tragically Hip or the Barenaked Ladies. I memorized their songs and travelled around to watch them play in muddy fields. I camped and cottaged and I drank good Canadian beer from ice-chilled bottles. By dating those who were either white or who lived the same way, I became an honorary member of the white world of high school—the really popular people. In this world, everyone just forgot that I looked completely different.

I chose my black and white moments in high school based on convenience and circumstances. Stanley Cup season, Winter Olympics: White. Final Four, NBA Finals, Summer Olympics:

Black. I lived my life on this social equator because I secretly loved rock music and acoustic guitars and camping outdoors and baseball, and because I hated the stereotype attributed to black women—the finger- and head-waving attitude. I tried not to get angry and I tried not to be too white. I didn't want to be a crazy, black woman or a white-on-the-inside Oreo.

In those difficult moments when I was forced to make a definitive social choice in public, like any time I entered the cafeteria or when Lorraine West came to Littlepalooza, I would wish that the earth would open up and let me fall into the heart of its red-hot lava. Because there was no way to win and there were so many ways to lose by stuffing my irregular form into other people's narrow boxes.

Matt Little held backyard beer parties every summer in high school. The most famous bash was an annual event he named Littlepalooza. Everyone who attended Matt's parties was either white or, like me, had chosen the white world of high school. It was a big and elaborate event, mostly because underage drinking was permitted. It always produced ridiculous stories of adolescent drunkenness—like the time a guy passed out in the Littles' garden where he was discovered the next morning.

"Why do they invite you? Why don't they ever invite me?" Lorraine once asked when I mentioned the upcoming party.

Lorraine didn't drink and she didn't like rock music. I figured she wouldn't like it. Only the real reason I never invited her to come along was that I didn't want her there. I was worried about what would happen when my two worlds collided. In the summer leading up to our graduating year, it happened. I brought Lorraine West to Matt Little's party.

Lorraine and I walked into Matt's backyard as the sun dropped below the low branches, the round, gold glow creating a pink sky beyond the fence line. Burgers sizzled on the grill. Beer and drinks chilled in coolers. Insects buzzed noisily against the porch lights. The Tragically Hip blasted from speakers that were facing the screen door from inside the family room.

I had never bought a Hip album, but I knew the lyrics of every one of their songs, because my friends were devoted followers. They bought their albums the day they were released and held parties to celebrate, downing shots together at the start of every new song in celebration. When certain songs came on, the boys would all gather in the centre of the yard, arms wrapped around each other. They would sing at the top of their lungs, heads huddled together, beers toasting the moonlight as they finished.

Lorraine and I each grabbed a can of pop and sat down at a brown picnic table that was set on square, grey yard stones. Dan Noble made his way over and sat down beside me. Dan played for our high school football team on the defensive line. He was thick with broad shoulders and fair skin spotted in brown freckles. Lorraine was facing him, her head tilted away from the speakers, fingers near her eardrums. Dan looked over at me and I tried to smile as we both watched her struggle in her obvious discomfort. *Just pretend you like it.* I had been doing it for so long, it was second nature. I had actually started to like the Hip's unique musicality.

Lorraine asked if Dan and I hung out often. She and I hadn't been spending much time together. I knew she was conducting her own research. Dan and I both shrugged, the music filling in the long silence. I told Lorraine that I was working a lot that summer, travelling with my soccer team. But the truth was I had started to choose my white friends more consistently, more often. For reasons I didn't yet understand, it felt easier, less awkward.

Dan told Lorraine about a trip we had all made to a cottage on the May long weekend. He told her about the cold, about the rock and mossy island where we set up our tents, where we slept in sweatsuits and hats and mittens because of the below-seasonal temperatures. He told her about the keg of cheap beer we forced ourselves to drink, and Lorraine nodded. She sipped her soda, silently judging. A Hip song about New Orleans danced out of the speakers.

"Would you ever date a black girl?" Lorraine asked Dan, eyes fixed on him, catching his reaction.

I slumped with resignation as words about sinking and swimming bellowed around us. I used my fingers to play the drums on the picnic table. Dan turned towards me and I looked away, tapping the wood with the balls of my fingers. As my fingers moved to the beat, I thought about how difficult it was to drum. It was hard to maintain more than one rhythm simultaneously.

"I don't know," Dan said.

Lorraine scowled. "What do you mean you don't know?"

Dan shrugged. He searched for eye contact with me, again unsuccessfully.

"Of course," he answered with extended hesitation.

By choosing the open-minded approach, Dan hoped he was safe. But I knew better. Lorraine was just lining up her arsenal.

"Do you even find black women attractive?"

I could almost hear Dan whisper *help me* in the pause that followed. I watched the flies buzzing against the sky, and continued to drum more quickly, almost frantically.

"Of course," he said again, slower.

"Really?" she said, as though she could detect lies, because she had discovered one and wanted him to know she knew better. She wanted to give him a chance to redeem himself, before she buried him.

"Beyoncé's hot," he said shrugging.

I stopped drumming and shook my head, as I gazed down into the dark hole of my empty can of soda.

Lorraine rolled her eyes and muttered, "Typical."

Dan looked perplexed and I tried to apologize—for not helping, for bringing her, for doing nothing. I tried to explain as I looked over at him, but I knew she wasn't finished.

"That's because she's light. That's because she practically looks white. All men think Beyoncé's beautiful. What about Kelly Rowland—do you think she's attractive?"

Dan sat there stone-faced and silent as the Hip sang about muddy memories. I sang along with them, my lips moving, my fingers tapping, until Lorraine turned to me, venomous.

"Seriously, how can you listen to this music?"

I treated the question as rhetorical, which is the only way to win with her—to let her anger sink her ship of personal frustrations. I bobbed to the beat as the chorus faded in the distance.

Lorraine never came to one of Matt's parties again. But later that year, Dan and I went out on a few dates. Even though I look nothing like Beyoncé.

I didn't realize until much later how much Lorraine and I actually had in common—how much the choices I was making were done to avoid bigger issues.

Lorraine used to say that she wanted to date a white guy. She said it was because she was tired of black men who didn't treat her well. Only I don't think that was the real reason. I think she believed that if a decent-looking white guy said so, she could really be beautiful. Because at the core of all our conflicts was her belief that light-skinned women were more attractive.

It's why she wanted curly hair, like mine, even when hers was admired. It's why she wanted to come to Littlepalooza, where white-guy options were more plentiful. It's why she asked Dan those questions. What she wanted to know, and what I wanted to know too, was can I be beautiful?

If a white guy said that out of all the potential magazine-cover white girls who were walking around the school he would rather have you, you were really special—unequivocally, universally beautiful. Dark, fair or otherwise.

When you believe that real beauty is outside your genetic possibilities, as I came to accept from the things I saw around me, on TV, and in magazines, having a white boyfriend was a way of proving that what I saw was thankfully and grossly inaccurate. I was beautiful because he said so. I didn't understand how distorted that thinking was until I fell for a white guy in university—until the problems of my social chameleon lifestyle unravelled in a mess of brokenness and confusion.

Martin and I met during our first week on campus, where we lip-synched a boy-girl pop duet on a set of speakers in a circular pub on campus. We moved and turned, bodies locked, differences in motion—a hand-holding, official item soon after. We had a lot in common—friends, faith, music, famous football fathers. And because he was white and popular, I felt lost in acceptance—delighted and beautiful.

Only soon after we started dating, something stirred me with discomfort. I started to sense the differences between us. He had black friends and poorly imitated their accents and their expressions in order to be more like them. He didn't notice the subtle black stereotypes he projected in his words, he didn't see them in films, or on television. He loved the way my body curved. He loved the way my frizzy hair felt. He often called it fuzzy. He melted whenever I straightened it like the white girls in my residence.

Martin looked at me in a way that acknowledged my blackness and his distinct whiteness, and he didn't even know it. He compared tans in a way that implied blackness could be achieved via sunlight. He saw the world with a blind ignorance he couldn't see and I couldn't explain, because I saw a world saturated in heavy white light, where I was always part of the shadows.

In a playwriting class that I took some time after we broke up, I was asked to write a play about something that was important. I wrote about Martin—about my white friends and my black friends, about a black girl who couldn't figure herself out.

To infuse us with ideas and to help us get started, our professor asked us to find a spot around the theatre. She gave us an object or a word to help each of us unravel an impromptu monologue—something from the gut, from the belly of our main character's secret hang-ups.

A well, my professor said to me as she tapped me on the shoulder.

I thought of a well—that deep, bottomless blackness wrapped in stones that dripped of mouldy residue. I thought of how dirty it was. I thought about how perfect, clean, and free of error the colour white is, of how black is always sin and bad and wicked. I revealed how ugly and angry and wicked I felt when people used the word "black" to describe me.

I rambled until I was weeping about all the things I never wanted to say—about wanting to be white and date white so I would never feel what the word *black* meant, about my resentment towards Lorraine, about how ashamed I was of black people who got angry over everything. I wanted black people to show restraint, even when they were right, because I didn't understand where their anger came from. I didn't realize that that anger was inside of me also.

It was the first time I understood that what happened in the past, the history of black people in America, had left a residue of hurt inside of me. It was the first time the shadow of history stormed out from a deeper part of me, reminding me of all of the things that had shaped the way I saw myself.

9

I ATTENDED a conference in St. Louis, Missouri, with my husband, Mark, soon after I graduated from university. We stopped at a convenience store in a popular, posh hotel to get a drink. As we walked through the store, the woman at the cash register began a conversation with us. She was white and in her mid-forties, with short, curly hair. She was wearing a long, shapeless, floral dress. Wood and bead necklaces dangled against her chest. She asked us where we were from, what we were doing in the city, and how we liked St. Louis. She asked us what it was like to live in Canada.

"How did you get out?" she said eventually. Meaning out of the projects, poverty, out of the life she saw people who looked like us living on the other side of the river—a disadvantaged, historically black neighbourhood known as East St. Louis.

She had a friend who lived there and she wanted him to move to her neighbourhood, a neighbourhood that was better for his children, safer. But he didn't want to do it, she said. Or he didn't know how. And she sat there by her cash register waiting for our explanation, hoping we could help her. *How did you get out?*

I paused for a minute, looked at Mark, then said what was true for both of us.

"In Canada, you don't have to get out," I told her. "We were born out, I suppose. We live in a mixed neighbourhood. We're not poor. It's different."

Only I couldn't explain what I meant, and she didn't understand what I was saying. So I told her what I knew of my father's story at the time—about starting in the projects, going to college, about moving to Canada. I explained what little I knew of it.

Sometime later, when I asked my father to tell me his getting-out story, he didn't understand the question.

"How did you escape life in the North End?" I asked.

Escape, my father said, was far too dramatic. "It wasn't a big deal," he told me.

By the time my father was a senior at Notre Dame High School, Bryant, his stepbrother, was a toddler. My grandmother was working at a job that paid very little. George Spaulding was hardly around anymore.

"What were your plans? What were you going to do?" I asked him.

My father placed his feet on the coffee table and crossed them at the ankles. He leaned back into the pillow behind his head. On the TV, CNN commentators were discussing Barack Obama's first few days in office.

"I wanted to do what Larry did. I wanted to get a scholarship," he told me. "I kind of knew that if I got away, if I went away to school, that I probably wouldn't come back to Portsmouth. It's kind of the thing that you knew."

Know was a tricky word when it came to my father. It required more specifics. There was *know* as in: everyday *know*ledge, an obvious reality for everyone. Then there was *know*, as in divine intuition.

"How did you know that?"

"A lot of the kids who left for football or sports, who went away to university—you realized none of them came back," he said. He took his glasses off and wiped the lenses with the bottom of his shirt. "There wasn't much opportunity in Portsmouth. Somehow I knew that if I got out, I wasn't coming back."

I nodded. *Know*, as in intuition—an instinctive awareness of things not seen or known by others.

My father wanted to get out of Portsmouth, because he realized that people who went away didn't come back. There was something bigger out there. He had never travelled more than a few hours from town, and he didn't know much about places that existed beyond his neighbourhood. But something inside of him was following that Norfolk & Western train out of Portsmouth to a destination he couldn't see or imagine—on the heels of a man named Larry Hisle.

When I was eleven, I was a devoted fan of the Toronto Blue Jays—particularly Joe Carter, one of the team's best outfielders. I cut out articles about him from the newspaper, and I bought magazines that contained stories about his life on and off the baseball field. I glued the stories into a scrapbook I kept in the top drawer of a desk in my bedroom.

When my father noticed my interest, he started to take me to Blue Jay games. Only he never bought tickets. He would ask me if I wanted to go to a game, and if I said yes he would say, "Okay, I'll call Larry." Next thing I knew, we were sitting behind home plate, next to the wives and kids of players like Kelly Gruber and John Olerud.

I would wear the No. 29 Joe Carter jersey my parents got me for Christmas, and after the game my father would lead me to an elevator that was monitored by a security officer. He would give his name to the guard, who would scroll down a list before opening elevator doors where another security officer—seated on a bar chair—would take us to the lowest level of the stadium.

The basement of the SkyDome was a grey tunnel with asphalt floors that was windowless and dark, even in the daytime. It was filled with equipment, staff, and coaches from both teams, along with the kids and wives who had sat by us during the game, who were waiting for their fathers and husbands, respectively.

My father and I would stand to the side and lean against the grey walls of the tunnel as players and coaches emerged from a set of large, blue doors. It was like being in the arrivals section at the airport, except that these people had been on the baseball field and on television moments earlier. I watched for Joe Carter while my father looked for Larry Hisle—the Jays batting coach and my father's old friend from the North End.

The first time I met Larry in the SkyDome tunnel, he shook my hand and smiled as my father introduced us—a toothy grin that showed bright, white teeth beneath a thick, dark moustache. He looked at me and smiled as though honoured by the introduction.

"Me and your father go way back," he told me, as he leaned over to get a better look at me. "She looks just like you, Chuck," he said, smiling.

My father nodded down at me.

I smiled as well as I could, because I was nervous and unsure; because I didn't yet know about the North End or charley-horse tag or games played with insects, raw beans, or Popsicle sticks; because I didn't understand who Larry was.

When I finally spotted Joe Carter, I tugged on my father's arm and squealed as quietly as I could manage. Larry waved him over. Joe was out of uniform, wearing a white windbreaker-type tracksuit. I was star-struck as he shook my father's hand before bending down to shake mine. Larry asked if I wanted to take a photo with Joe, and I nodded. I handed my camera to my father as Joe Carter wrapped his arms around my small shoulders.

I decided right there that Larry Hisle was my most favourite friend of my father's.

What I remember now about that meeting beneath the Sky-Dome, and the ones that would follow, has little to do with meeting major league baseball players. When I think about those encounters with Larry Hisle now, I remember how my father changed when he was around his old friend from the projects, how an accent emerged that was strong and familiar, how his voice cracked with laughter that came from deep within his belly, as the two of them remembered old North End stories. I remember looking up and watching my father's face as he and Larry spoke. I remember seeing a rare kind of happy. Fifteen years would pass before I came to understand why Larry Hisle meant so much to my father.

Claudine Hisle named her only child Larry Eugene Hisle after Larry Eugene Doby—one of America's first black professional baseball players. At an early age, the name proved fitting. Larry was a phenomenal athlete. While Claudine, an avid baseball fan, would push him in the direction of the game she loved, a game in which he thrived, her son would dream of playing another sport professionally. Larry Hisle would spend his days in the North End aspiring for a basketball scholarship at Ohio University, a few hours away in the city of Athens.

When Larry was ten, his father suffered a brain aneurysm, which left Jupiter Hisle permanently hospitalized. The injury from the aneurysm was so severe that Larry's father would never again recognize him. Larry and his mother would struggle in Jupiter's absence; their phone would get cut off and their only working toilet would break down. Eventually, the city would shut off their water.

"But I was the happiest kid on earth," Larry told me, when I called him a few months after my visit to Portsmouth. "My mother and I would often take rides up to the top of the hill in Portsmouth. She said, 'Larry, you will one day live like these people.' I never knew what she was talking about, but I now know that she was instilling in me a will to settle for nothing less than the absolute best that life had to offer."

Eight months after Larry's father became ill, Larry's mother visited the hospital with symptoms from a mild, nagging illness. She was diagnosed with a kidney infection. Although kidney infections are typically not life-threatening, Claudine Hisle's case became fatal. Five days later, in the same hospital where Larry's father remained incapacitated, Larry's mother passed away. Relatives and local families helped care for the young boy. A few years later, when Larry's father also died, a family in Portsmouth formally adopted him.

Despite his hardships, Larry continued to excel in sports, chasing my father around the North End, playing baseball, and beating my father regularly in basketball. They would play a game called "24," in which the winner was the first person to get twenty-four points; my father was given twenty free points as a head start. Three years older than my father, Larry was always victorious.

In 1967, Larry secured a basketball scholarship to Ohio University. Two weeks before classes were scheduled to begin at OU, Larry agreed to meet with the owner of the Philadelphia Phillies. A few days after the meeting, Larry revoked his scholarship and signed a contract with the major league ball club.

"I knew that that was what my mother would have wanted me to do," he told me. "She loved baseball."

I sensed a devout love for his mother, an ache for her that still plagued him as he spoke about her. It reminded me of the way my father swallowed back tears when he gave the eulogy at my grandmother's funeral, his longing for her to have witnessed significant moments, like the time he was honoured for his accomplishments in Portsmouth, or when each of his grandchildren was born and he held them in the hospital.

I was six months pregnant by the time Larry and I spoke, and he told me about his mother. As he talked, I pressed my hand against the little boy who was moving rapidly inside of me. I prayed I would see more of his life than Claudine Hisle and my grandmother had seen of their sons' lives. I prayed for the ability to teach my son the important lessons those women had instilled in their sons at a time when they had so much less and things were much more difficult.

On April 4, 1968, at a hotel in Memphis, Tennessee, a bullet from the rifle of escaped convict James Earl Ray struck Dr. Martin Luther King Jr. in the neck as he stood with the Reverend Jesse Jackson on the balcony of the Lorraine Motel. My father was at school in his senior year at Notre Dame High School. Larry was preparing for his first game with the Philadelphia Phillies.

When news of King's death reached the public, riots broke out across the country. They took place in over a hundred and fifty cities and resulted in the deaths of thirty-nine people, thirty-four of them black. Over 22,000 federal troops and 34,000 National Guardsmen were sent to aid local police in the destruction and devastation that resulted from five days of rioting—the largest amount of aid ever called on to deal with a domestic civil disturbance.

As riots erupted across the country following King's death, my father and his classmates gathered solemnly on the front steps of Notre Dame High School. Nuns tied black bands on their arms as the crowd of youngsters spoke in whispers. Some muffled tears, others shifted awkwardly and uneasily.

My father held a large, wooden cross in his hand, flanked by Al and Gerald. The rest of the students moved forward in slow unison behind the three, black seniors; they stepped in cue as Portsmouth residents watched from their porches. The sombre arm bands, the hollow footsteps, the despondent white faces, the three black boys, and the wooden cross must have inspired an eerie silence that grey day in April as the students of Notre Dame High School headed down the hill and across the train tracks to a memorial service held in a North End church for Martin Luther King Jr.

"Of all the people who have graced our nation, no one had more of an impact on America than Martin Luther King Jr.," Larry told me when he recalled the day his major league debut was postponed on account of the assassination and the ensuing riots. "When his life was taken, it was as if they had ripped out a part of my heart. This man, more than any other man, had worked tire-lessly to make life better in this country—not only for blacks but for everyone who was disadvantaged."

The autopsy that followed the assassination of Dr. King revealed a heart that was decades older than the thirty-nine-year-old orator. It confirmed Coretta Scott King's suspicions of her husband's depression. Despite his eloquence and passion for peaceful protest, the injustice he saw and the racism he encoun-tered had not only led to his untimely death, it had also broken his heart.

What I started to wonder, as I thought of Dr. King, was how my father endured the heartache, how he overcame the anger and depression. It seemed that the adversity my father encoun-tered, and the challenges that would follow, somehow made him stronger.

10

EOPLE call our family religious because my mother leads a Bible study group; because my brother is in ministry; because I pray openly before meals and advocate faith in the best and worst circumstances. Growing up, I never quite knew what my father believed entirely—whether he came to church for my mother's sake, sent us to a Christian school for the uniforms, or carried a Bible when he spoke at Christian camps because it was expected. His faith was one more item in the list of things I didn't really know about my father. It was also the thing that, when I discovered what really happened and the order of events, significantly changed the way I saw my father.

I knew my father went to Notre Dame, but I never saw him do that forehead-shoulder thing with his finger. I didn't think it had anything to do with religion. I never heard him talk about the Pope or the Virgin Mary. So growing up, I assumed Notre Dame High School recruited my father to play sports. I figured it was some kind of program developed by the administration to take advantage of desegregation—an outreach initiative layered in all kinds of ulterior motives.

"Recruit me?" my father said with a scowl when I asked him how he ended up at Notre Dame instead of the local public school. "I went there because I was Catholic."

"You're Catholic?"

I made a decision that God was real when I was quite young, based on what I'd heard from my mother and what I sensed somewhere deep inside me. I knew my numbers, my letters, I knew right and wrong—that you obeyed your elders, didn't lie. I knew that you didn't steal bubble gum, even when there were open containers at the convenience store, even when no one would notice. I figured someone must have made those perfect stars that lit the darkness, stars that always left me speechless.

So with my mother at my bedside one night, I prayed the prayer that would label me a Protestant going forward. I said that I believed in one God who sent His own holy Son just for me to get to heaven. When I said Amen, through joyful tears, my mother told me that angels were celebrating at a party held in my honour. I couldn't go to the party, but that night I dreamt of clouds and feathered wings, coloured balloons, and yellow cake with chocolate frosting.

In the church I attended, people got baptized when they were older, when they were old enough to say that believing in God was their individual choice and they were ready to make that declaration public. I was sixteen when I stood in front of a congregation of friends, family, and strangers and said that I believed in God. I wasn't ashamed to admit it. My pastor dunked me in swirls of clear, cold water while my father sat next to my mother and watched from the pews in the massive sanctuary. When he lifted me up out of the water, white robe wet and heavy, I prayed that my father would come to know God like the rest of our family. Only faith was important to my father from the very beginning.

"I was eight or nine when I got baptized in the Baptist Church," my father told me. "Old churches in the States, they would ask you for a point of faith"—they would ask if you believed in God—"and if you said yes they would take you and put you in a robe and baptize you right there. They wouldn't waste any time," he said.

For my father, the water was only the beginning. After he was baptized, he continued to have questions about life and death, and about God, questions that led him to a Catholic priest in Portsmouth. He converted to Catholicism, and at the age of ten, transferred to the Catholic middle school that filtered into Notre Dame High School. My father would attend the private Catholic high school which was under the direction of headmaster Father Grimes, instead of attending Portsmouth High School like the majority of the kids in the North End.

In spite of Notre Dame's academic rigour and spiritual foundation—or maybe in light of it—my father would thrive. He would lead the Notre Dame Titans to an impressive football legacy—each game preceded by solemn ritual.

White sport socks sweep the Notre Dame floors as the team of boys exit the gymnasium and walk towards the room at the end of the long, burgundy-floor hallway—shiny tiles glistening under the glimmer of afternoon sunshine. The only sound that passes between boys is the whisper that follows their motion. Through the doors up ahead a large, wooden cross with a nail-pierced-palms-and-feet Jesus hangs on the white walls of the chapel.

The boys enter the room and file into rows of lacquered wood pews. Tall, narrow windows with bold lines and coloured glass re-create holy scenes and the saintly acts of pious figures like Paul, Mark, and Thomas Aquinas. A Bible sits open on a podium, light perched overtop, candles accompanying it with tiny, orange flickers.

The boys kneel, heads hung low over clasped fingers. My father bends over the front row and prays silently along with his teammates. He prays for his family—for Bryant and his mother, for his relatives, for people he knows in the North End who aren't well. He prays for the future, for what lies ahead. Then he turns his thoughts to the game that's looming closer. He imagines the scoreboard and hopes for victory. He pictures the win, the passes, the catches, the runs into the end zone. When he feels a tap on his shoulder, he stands and heads back down the aisle, out of the chapel, and down the slippery hallway. He follows the team back to the gymnasium where they relace their shoes in the silence that continues all the way to the buses that are waiting to take them to the stadium.

My father took us to Notre Dame High School during our visit to Portsmouth, when the entire school was preparing for the homecoming pep rally. *Home of the Notre Dame Titans* was painted over the entryway to the gymnasium. Inside the gym, two large frames were hung high on the wall over the physical education offices. In one was my father's Notre Dame High School navy jersey. In the other, an autographed picture of him in his college uniform. A banner nearby on the very same wall commemorated the 1967 State Champion football team.

Students in navy and white school uniforms, some covered with a football jersey, filed into the gymnasium and sat on the bleachers for a series of presentations that included one from my father. When the assembly was finished and most of the crowd had returned to their classes, a few of the boys in football jerseys stayed back, standing nearby, hesitating awkwardly. Finally, one boy walked over to my father while the others watched from a distance.

"Mr. Ealey, there's a rule here at Notre Dame." He pointed to the frames on the wall. "If any student hits those, the person who threw the ball has to sit out for the game. They have to sit out for the whole class."

My father smiled, laughed a little. The young man relaxed his shoulders, and grinned back at him.

"Did you ever hit it?" my father said.

The young man shook his head emphatically. "No, sir. I've never hit your picture. Never."

My father signed the jersey, and when the young man was done, the others boys stepped closer and handed my father their jerseys to sign.

In his final year at Notre Dame in 1967, my father's team had a perfect record—twenty-seven wins and zero losses. They were named State Champions, which was a monumental accomplishment for a school of their size and in their area. My father and Headmaster Father Grimes hoped that the team's record would entice a college team to offer him a full scholarship at quarterback.

At the end of the season, my father was approached by three universities in Ohio—Miami University in Oxford, the University of Dayton, and Ohio University in Athens. They contacted him through Father Grimes because there were no phones in the projects. In February 1968, my father went to visit Dayton and Miami University; he also sat down with the head coaches at Ohio University. None of the schools offered him a full scholarship and the chance to play quarterback; they all talked about a scholarship to play defensive end. My father rejected all three offers.

"Why would you do that?" I asked him.

"I wanted to play quarterback," he told me.

"But what were you planning to do? How were you going to get an education?"

"I thought I would join the military."

I shuddered. The only way my father could have afforded an education was by joining the army. I asked my father why he didn't just accept the offers and work his way to quarterback when he got there.

My father just repeated his answer. "I wanted to play quarterback."

In 1975, the *American Journal of Sports Medicine* published an article about a study that investigated the sociological connections between race and positions in football—a study conducted around the time my father spoke with the three Ohio university coaches. I found a photocopy of the article in a box of old papers in my parents' basement. It was highlighted and scribbled with my sister's notations from a project she had done in university where she studied kinesiology—the science of sport and human movement.

The article proposed that in the sixties, American football coaches were matching racial stereotypes with "demand characteristics" when they determined suitability for various positions on the football field. Coaches were assigning a disproportionate number of players to certain athletic positions on the premise that the role demanded skills and characteristics that were dominant in one racial group and weaker in another.

The article identified three white positions: quarterback, offensive guard, and centre; and three black positions: running back, wide receiver, and defensive back. In American high schools, the ratio of black to white players in black positions was fairly even, 27:25; but the ratio of black to white players in white positions was a disproportionate 4:31. In the college sample, the statistics were still even for the black positions, but for the white positions, the ratio for black to white players was 3:70.

The most prominent and obvious disparity was discovered in the quarterback position where a high level of intellect, leadership, and the capacity for careful analysis were necessities— qualities that, according to white American coaches, black men were inherently lacking.

By the spring of 1968, Headmaster Father Grimes was concerned about his senior quarterback's prospects. He put in a call to an old friend at the University of Toledo. Grimes explained that although the football season was over, and although no one from Toledo had looked at his players because Portsmouth was so much further south than they typically recruited, he had a quarterback who was really something.

That March, my father was called down to the headmaster's office where he was introduced to the University of Toledo's assistant football coach, Dick Walker.

My father has massive hands and long fingers, which, when I was younger, he used during handshakes to grade the young men who came to visit my sister and me. Handshakes reflect character and confidence, and can be used to gauge self-assurance. Not too weak or limp, and not sweaty, my father would say. Whenever my sister and I felt strongly for someone, we gave them sufficient warning. We prepared them. Shake his hand well, we told them. Shake it good and hard.

I wondered what Coach Walker learned about my father from his handshake, what he saw in the round eyes of the undefeated, black quarterback from the projects at that private Catholic school in Portsmouth.

"Son, do you know where Toledo is?" Coach Walker said.

My father shook his head. "No, sir."

Before he visited Miami University and Ohio University— one on the east side of the state, the other on the west—my father had rarely travelled farther than Columbus, the capital of Ohio, one hour west of Portsmouth. Toledo was five hours north, near Lake Erie, close to the Canadian border.

That night, with the football season long over, Coach Dick Walker and Father Grimes attended my father's final basketball game of the season.

When my father's classmates recounted stories in Mary Barry's kitchen, they recalled the infamous basketball game that Coach Dick Walker and Father Grimes watched in the gymnasium at Notre Dame High School. It had become one of those tall tales his classmates told repeatedly when they found themselves together. According to my father, the story had morphed into a memory that was infinitely larger than its original unfolding.

The basketball game pitted Notre Dame's Coach Miller against his brother's team from Wheelersburg. It was a close and evenly matched basketball game. With one minute left to play, the score was tied. With just under twenty seconds left on the clock, the Wheelersburg point guard drove towards the basket to put Wheelersburg up by one, with four seconds remaining.

Notre Dame called a timeout and Coach Miller drew up a play. When the whistle blew and the clock started, my father caught the ball and dribbled towards the baseline. He shot the ball as time ticked down to zero. The ball slipped through the net as the final buzzer blared. Wheelersburg fans stared at the scoreboard in dismay; Notre Dame fans celebrated. My father's last shot in his final high school basketball game secured a Titans victory.

Some of my father's Notre Dame classmates said he shot from half court, others said he was at least a few feet away from three-point range. Regardless of what they remembered, all of them agreed that it was incredible to watch, that they would never forget that moment. As his classmates recounted that night, my father said:

"It didn't quite happen like that. No, no, it didn't happen like that," he told me.

My father told me later that it was just your normal, every-day buzzer-beater. Although I don't know anyone who thinks "normal" and "everyday" are words that go with game-winning buzzer-beaters. Coach Walker must have agreed with me, because after the game he approached my father and made plans for him to travel up to the University of Toledo to see the campus and to meet with the head coach, Frank Lauterbur.

"I don't know what kind of a football player he is, but he's some kind of athlete," Coach Walker would tell Lauterbur.

My father drove up to the University of Toledo campus in the spring of 1968 with Notre Dame teammate Jim Goodman. Goodman—a strong, heavyset linebacker—had already been offered a full scholarship to Miami University. He planned to accept the offer from Miami when he got back, but he went to Toledo with my father because he enjoyed the pampering of recruiters.

As they drove onto the campus, my father stared out the car window. He marvelled at the old clock tower and the urban bustle. He liked the beige stone buildings and the bridges that connected curving pathways; he liked the tall trees and green hedges that lined the walkways. It looked different from the Miami University and University of Dayton campuses. It was stately and prestigious. My father liked it immediately.

The two high school recruits from Portsmouth were each assigned to veterans who would serve as hosts during the weekend visit. They would show my father and Jim a good time in an effort to entice them to choose Toledo. On the visits to Dayton and Oxford, my father had been assigned veterans who were black. He was taken to black bars with black teammates, where he celebrated with black students and black locals. But in Toledo, things were different.

"I was taken out by Bob Flynn, who was a white guy," my father told me. "We went to a city bar."

I asked if it was the first time my father had been served a drink in a bar that was integrated, but he couldn't remember. He just remembered that from the start he liked Toledo.

By the time my father visited the University of Toledo that spring, Frank Lauterbur had been head coach of the Toledo Rockets for five years. Initially he struggled, his record mediocre, even shoddy; but it takes four years to see what a coach is capable of— when the team is stocked with his own recruits who have been trained under his leadership.

In Lauterbur's fourth year with Toledo, the Rockets won the Mid-American Conference Championship. A few months later, Lauterbur was sitting across from an unlikely pair of recruits from a small, private Catholic school in southern Ohio. A journalist from *The Blade*, Toledo's local paper, asked Frank Lauterbur, years later, about that meeting.

"The principal at Portsmouth Notre Dame . . . said they had a real fine quarterback who had been undefeated for three years. His name was Chuck Ealey and the priest told me that Bo [Schembechler, the Miami of Ohio coach] and Bill Hess [Ohio U] were looking at him. . . . Dick [Walker] said, 'I don't know what kind of a football player he is, but he's about as good an athlete as I've ever seen.' So we arranged a visit. This big tackle, Jim

Goodman, came up with Chuck, they're sitting in my office, and I said, 'I've got scholarships for both of you.' I'd never seen film of either kid, I'd never seen either of them play. I offered them scholarships sight unseen and told Chuck that he'd be a quarterback at Toledo. He hadn't gotten that assurance from other schools. Made me look pretty smart, eh?"[1]

With two months left in their senior year, Jim Goodman and my father both received offers to play at the University of Toledo on full scholarship—Goodman at guard and my father at quarterback. My father accepted the offer immediately. Goodman would turn down his offer from Miami University and accept Toledo's offer.

Coach Lauterbur had never seen my father play football, but his instincts would prove monumental for the school and my father. When my father left the North End in the summer of 1968 for the University of Toledo, he would never again live in the projects.

My father doesn't remember much about the day he left for Toledo. He left Portsmouth soon after high school was over to begin training on campus, and to start a job he had secured with a Toledo trucking company.

Before he left, he spent some time with his brother who, in the summer of '68, was just three years old. Maybe my father took Bryant out to the field near their complex where the bigger boys played. Maybe he watched Bryant march through the grass, the green blades flat under the weight of his stomping. Maybe my father brought his football with him and played with Bryant one last time before he left the North End. *Keep your eye on the ball*, my father would say. The little boy would hold out his hands, palms outstretched, eyes closed, giggling.

I often try to imagine my grandmother and Bryant on that hot June day—what they felt as they squeezed my father tightly.

I imagine my grandmother prayed and gripped him until she really had to let go. I imagine her face was wet from crying. Tears must have rolled down Bryant's face as he said goodbye to his brother, the only man who had consistently loved him. I picture the little boy's outstretched arms as my father opens the driver's door, slides in, and starts the engine.

I'm sure my father looked down the road instead of turning back to see his brother because he doesn't like to cry, ever. I imagine he waved as he drove forward, and that his eyes watered as the silhouette of the little boy disappeared behind him. I imagine Bryant pressed his salty-wet face into the bosom of my grandmother, that they held onto one another and cried and cried. *Junior! Junior!*

TOLEDO
1968–1972

The ultimate measure of a man is not
where he stands in moments of comfort
and convenience, but where he stands at
times of challenge and controversy.

MARTIN LUTHER KING JR.

11

THERE'S A CITY named Toledo in Spain, but the Toledo where my mother grew up and where my father attended college in the late sixties is the one located in northern Ohio. It's the fourth-largest city in the state, one hour from Detroit on Interstate 75 where the Maumee River runs off Lake Erie. It's known as the Glass City because of its historical innovation in the production of glass—a material that's virtually indestructible and can withstand the effects of nature's most powerful elements.

Other than the university, the local zoo, glass innovation, and the I-75 that forces Canadians to pass by the city on treks to Florida, there's not much else to see or talk about in Toledo. It's pretty forgettable. But in 1968, just a few months after Dr. King's assassination, my father's arrival in the city of indestructible glass seemed to have changed that for the better.

By the time I was able to drive and could go out with my friends more regularly, my father and I were rarely alone in the house without my mother. On those unusual occasions when my mother was away for an evening and I didn't have plans with friends, I would hole up in my bedroom while my father hunkered down in the basement to watch his favourite Vietnam War movie—a movie he had seen a dozen times, that no one ever wanted to watch with him, despite his petitions, because the movie was older than I was. We had bought him more recent Vietnam War blockbusters, movies we were willing to watch with him because we recognized the cast of actors featured in the trailers, but whenever he was alone he would watch that same film, filled with exuberance.

When I was home from university one weekend and my mother was at a conference, I felt the familiar vibration of the floors as machine guns and ammo rat-a-tat-tatted underneath my footsteps. I crept halfway down the stairs and sat on a step where I could watch him unseen through the railings. He was sitting a few feet away with a wooden bowl of popcorn and a large plastic cup filled with ice and soda. The backdrop of the television outlined his frame, and when he picked up his cup and took a sip I could hear the ice cubes crack and dance against the plastic. On the TV screen, men lumbered through dense jungles in darkness.

"What's going on?" I said.

My father turned his head slightly. He said the white guys were on a rescue mission; they were looking for another American soldier. The missing American appeared sporadically, but he didn't look like the others. His face was striped in black mud, and he was hiding in a cave of dangling vines and vegetation. He didn't look like he wanted to go back to America. Frankly, he didn't look like he was of sound mind. When I said this, my father laughed.

"The Vietnam War made everyone crazy. It made people crazy," he said, eyes fixed on the TV screen.

By the time my father headed to university in 1968, the number of Americans serving in Vietnam was estimated to be over 500,000—an increase from an initial count of 15,000 in the fifties. College students across the country started to take action against America's involvement. Anti-war organizations followed the government's operations and the nation's financial expenditures carefully, garnering support against the unpopular overseas conflict.

Someone once said that the Vietnam War is my father's war, because it's the war of his generation; because his early years were shaped by the conflict that divided the country and seemed never-ending. I disagree wholeheartedly.

The real war of that generation, for men who looked like my father, was taking place on American soil. It was a not-so-civil war that was easy to define but hard to resolve. It had been going on much longer than the Vietnam War and had its own alarming share of missing-in-action casualties. It was a war between black and white Americans, a war of civil injustices. It was the war I really wanted my father to talk about.

My father and I began to discuss his time at the University of Toledo the winter after my visit to Portsmouth, when it was crisp and cold outside. The orange flames in my parent's fireplace flared upwards as dry winds whirled and whistled against the windows. My father adjusted the pillows at one end of the couch and I sat on the other end, a blanket draped over my legs, my back against the arm, toes pointing towards him.

"What did you think when you first met your new teammates?"

My father looked towards the window, shrugged dismissively.

"Dad?"

"That was a long time ago," he said.

"But what do you remember?"

"Not much."

My father leaned his head back against the couch and stared at the white speckles on the ceiling.

"You have to remember something," I said.

I waited for a minute. Then another. I wondered if he talked with his old teammate Jim Goodman on campus or if things changed when they got to Toledo. I wondered if anyone discussed Dr. King's assassination or the civil rights movement, or Mohammad Ali—the undefeated heavyweight champion of the world who refused to serve in Vietnam, and said to a reporter, "I ain't got no quarrel with no Viet Cong, they never called me a nigger." I wondered if they talked about those things or if they pretended it wasn't happening.

"Did the white and black guys hang out together?" I asked.

"The black guys were from different backgrounds," my father said. "Guys with great big Afros from Cleveland or Detroit. It was right in the heart of the civil rights movement."

The Afro was trendy among urban, black Americans, but my father had never seen Afros like the kind he saw in Toledo back in small-town Portsmouth. Mel Long, Al Baker, Ronnie Roberts, and John Saunders—black teammates who would become my father's closest college friends—all had one. Donnie Fletcher from Detroit wore black clothes and dark sunglasses; my father said he had a *serious* Afro. My father had only seen Afros like that on television.

"I could see, okay, we've got some issues here. We were not on the same page in principle. I was looking at it going, this is *different*."

I asked him about the white guys on the team and he shrugged, nonchalantly.

"All of the guys from farm fields were white guys," he told me.

What caught my father off guard when he arrived in Toledo were the differences he saw in his black teammates. The white teammates didn't concern him, because they were similar to his classmates from Portsmouth.

It reminded me of my own experiences in high school—the differences I felt between my black classmates and me. I wanted to know more about what happened those first days and who my father eventually connected with, but my father said that that was all he could remember. I asked him if someone else might remember more from those days, expecting him to direct me to Al Baker or Mel Long, because John Saunders had recently died and I hadn't heard of Donnie Fletcher or Ronnie Roberts.

Instead he said, "Don Fair would remember that kind of thing."

My mother, who was standing nearby in the kitchen, nodded in agreement. My father stood up and went to his office. When he returned, he handed me a piece of paper with a long-distance number on it.

In an old University of Toledo football magazine I found at my parents' house, there is a picture of Don Fair sitting in the front row of uniformed players in a No. 80 jersey, his dark hair combed in a wave that crossed his forehead, his sideburns cut short and trimmed, his pale, white hands placed casually on his kneecaps.

"It's been a long time since anyone asked me about those days. But I love talking about them," Don said when we spoke that January, a few months after my trip to Portsmouth.

He was living in Denver, Colorado, and from the start of our conversation I could hear his enthusiasm.

"What do you want to know?" he said.

I stared out the window of my office and watched cold smoke spin off my neighbour's frosted rooftop. I wrapped my finger between the spirals of the phone cord. I wanted to know what it was like for my father back then, what it was like to be black in America. I wanted to know all of the things my father couldn't remember. So I asked Don Fair to start at the beginning. I asked him if he remembered the first day of training camp or the first team meeting.

"That's the best question you could have asked," Don told me, laughing joyfully.

In the late sixties, senior players at the University of Toledo were called up for training camp a few days before the freshmen. The returning sophomores, juniors, and seniors who resided locally or outside Toledo all moved into Carter Hall East three weeks early. It was a multi-storey residence where the players would live throughout the school year. Don Fair's brother was a junior on the football team, so Don arrived on campus with his brother at the start of senior player practices in August 1968.

"We get up to Toledo, my brother and I," Don said. "It's late morning or early afternoon—a hot August day in Toledo. The freshmen are on the first floor, varsity are on the third floor. The varsity say, 'You guys got to meet down at the lunch hall,' which was the Rocket Room in Carter Hall. Well, the only other freshman who was there at the time was your dad. It was just me and him. So we go into the lunch hall with the rest of the guys. We don't know anybody so Chuck and I are kind of together and [Coach] Frank Lauterbur walks up and says, 'You guys need to go in the back.'

"Go in the back?" Don said, his tone echoing the confusion he felt on that day, his naiveté as a college freshman. "So we go in the back, into the kitchen, and they hand us an apron and a funny little paper hat. 'Put these on. You guys are serving the varsity lunch.'"

Don laughed, his voice vibrating as he finished the story.

"So your dad and I are serving the varsity lunch the first time we get to Toledo. 'Go get me some water. Go get me some

Kool-Aid, go.' You know, go do this and that. And we've got these funny hats on. Here we are thinking we're coming up to Toledo to play football. They let us know right away what our status was in life."

My father and Don Fair were part of the Toledo Rockets' Dirty Dozen in 1968, a term they gave to unsuspecting freshmen who were made to serve the senior players throughout training camp. Don remembered every detail.

Later that day, with no scheduled practices for rookies, my father and Don changed into workout clothes and headed out to an open field just outside of residence, across from the Glass Bowl Stadium.

My father rotates a football in his hands. He stretches out his long fingers and curls them around so the tips grip the texture of the leather. He pulls his arm back and launches the ball forward—a spiral that rises then falls towards Fair, who cradles the ball into his body.

"Where are you from?" Don asks.

"Portsmouth. You?" my father says.

"Canton originally."

Don tosses the ball back and it wobbles into my father's hands as they continue—back, forth, again, talking.

"What position they have you playing?" my father says.

"They recruited me as a defensive back. But I'm a wide receiver. You?"

Don tosses the ball back and my father takes a few steps forward to recover it.

"Quarterback," my father says.

They both stop and smile. Don jogs towards my father, and they line up in their proper roles. My father drops back, watches, waits, then throws the football, as Don runs in full stride and lets the ball fall right into him.

———————————

In football, wide receivers and quarterbacks are interconnected, the relationship between the two integral to any winning strategy. The connection that started that day between the white wide receiver from Canton and the black quarterback from Portsmouth outside Carter Hall marked the start of something important—two strangers from different worlds and backgrounds who became college football teammates at a critical point in history when friendships like theirs were rare and often frowned on.

I set my sights on securing an athletic scholarship to study in the United States like my father and my brother the year before I was going to graduate from high school. I was a competitive soccer player, and staying in Canada where you had to pay to go to school, in many ways, was equated with failure. It meant you weren't good enough. I wanted a scholarship because I wanted to prove to myself that I was talented enough to be sought after. I wanted to prove to my father that I wasn't just a good athlete—I was great like he was. Even if my father thought that soccer games were long and uneventful. "How can you like a sport that can end 0–0?" he would say to me.

I started contacting coaches at universities in Michigan and Ohio. I did my SATs; I sent them video footage. In the fall of 1998, a coach from the University of Toledo called me. I spoke with him for nearly an hour, and when I hung up the phone and told my father that they wanted me to visit, that there might be a partial scholarship and some funds to make up the difference, my father wasn't as excited as I thought he would be. He didn't congratulate me. He didn't reminisce about his days on campus or tell me where I should go for the best meals. He didn't offer to buy me a University of Toledo sweatshirt or lend me one of his. He just nodded with moderate enthusiasm.

When I asked him what he was thinking, what was wrong, he said carefully, "I'm not sure you'll like it."

I asked him what he meant, but he just shrugged and said, "America is different."

"What do you mean?"

"It's just different."

Damon was in the room, and said he agreed with our father, even though it would have meant being at the University of Toledo with my brother throughout my freshman year. It would have meant making all of those five-hour drives back and forth for holidays together.

Damon said that I wouldn't like going to Toledo, or study-ing in the States, not only because America was different, but because *I* was.

"It's still pretty divided. It's not like Canada," he told me.

I could hang out with the girls on the soccer team (most of whom were white), but when it came to hanging out or going out on weekends, it would be difficult for me to do things the way I had done them in high school—to have all white friends instead of black ones, to date guys who didn't look like me. Damon said that when I went to games in southern states, I might hear play-ers or fans call me names like the "N" word. I told him that was crazy. No one does that.

My father just sighed and murmured, "You have no idea."

Why would I?

We never followed up on that conversation and I never went to the University of Toledo, or pursued an American scholarship. Maybe they were right, after all. I didn't want to live where those kinds of things were expected of me. I had done too much of that in high school.

By the time March rolled around in my graduating year, I had received an early offer to a university I had seen in the small town of Guelph, Ontario. The UG soccer coaches urged me to come up a few weeks early for tryouts.

A few months later, I watched my mother drive away from the cracked cement curb in front of the Athletic Centre at the University of Guelph. My father didn't come with us because he had to work. Although, I'm not sure I even invited him. It was just tryouts, after all. There was a chance I would be coming home in a few days if I got cut. At least that's what I told him. I wouldn't return home until Thanksgiving.

In the front lobby of the Athletic Centre, a staff member gave me instructions on where to go to get ready. I was early. I headed down a narrow corridor to drop off my bags in the change room, sandals slipping along the grey film that coated the tiled hallway. Three men turned a corner and headed towards me. They stopped a yard in front of me, shoulder to shoulder, blocking the hallway. One of them asked if I was new here.

I looked around to see if they were talking to me, then nodded quickly. They all smiled, all black and model-buff handsome. One of them said something, but I didn't hear him exactly. Anxiety and thrill were zipping through my body like trapped flies looking for an exit. I wanted to appear self-assured, because confidence was dripping off their biceps. Only I couldn't get a word out.

"Are you a soccer player?" he said again. He had wide, full lips and perfectly straight teeth. He had a tiny waist and broad shoulders.

I nodded.

"Are you here for tryouts?"

"Yes." My voice sounded bumpy and awkward, my heart pumping so fast I felt out of breath just standing there. At least I had spoken.

"Good, good," he said. I could tell by the way his mouth rounded out words, the way his voice clicked against the back of his throat, fast and rhythmic, that he was Nigerian.

"What's your name?"

"Jael," I said slowly.

"Ja-el," he repeated.

He extended his hand. "Chinedu. But you can call me 'C.'" He pointed to the man in the middle, who had a small, lean build, who he introduced as Graham; then to the third member of their party, Scotty.

"We should let you get to practice," Graham said.

I chewed the corner of my lip. "Right."

Inside, my stomach fluttered, my body numb, immobile. Chinedu grabbed me around the shoulders and squeezed.

"Don't worry, girl, you'll be fine," he told me.

They told me to look out for a girl on the team named Leah. They said that she would be excited to meet me. "It should be easy to find her," they said.

Scotty and Graham stepped to one side to let me pass by them. I nodded and walked through the space they had made, headed towards the change room. When I got to the end of the hallway, my heavy bag strapped across my chest, I looked back at them. Scott and Graham were staring at a set of vending machines near the entryway, but Chinedu was standing slightly behind them, staring right back at me. He waved and smiled, so I waved and smiled back at him.

I wanted to run back and ask him questions. I wanted to know how many black people there were at the school and what they were like. I wanted to prepare myself. I wanted to know if he thought I would fit in at the University of Guelph, with people like him, even though I wasn't African or Caribbean. I wanted to know who Leah was.

I thought about that day later, how different it was from my first day of high school. I thought about all of the things I would learn at university, about my father and black history, starting that very first day when I found a friend in a young man named Chinedu.

Leah turned out to be the only other black girl on the team in my first year on the University of Guelph soccer team. We found each other easily and hit it off instantly, just as the boys predicted. She had hair that curled like mine, only tighter at the roots with sun-blonde streaks because she relaxed the ends and treated her hair to highlights. She'd grown up in Guelph and had had more white friends than I did. Because I wasn't of age, and because most of the bouncers couldn't tell us apart, I used her ID to get into parties.

As it turned out, Chinedu and Graham also played soccer; Scotty played football. They had a truckload of friends and pseudo-brothers from school and from their hometowns who were of all different backgrounds and races. I remained close with Chinedu and his roommates. I went to their parties and they came to visit me in residence occasionally. They treated me like a little sister and warned boys within earshot not to mess with me. Only that's not why our first meeting was particularly important.

Near the end of my first year of college, Chinedu and I were waiting in line in the cafeteria, perusing the menus posted on the dining hall chalkboard. I was looking for my meal card, fumbling through receipts and cards and coins in my wallet, when the plastic photo insert fell onto the ground. A picture of my parents was on top. My father was wearing a blue golf shirt, my mother in a green shirt and a floral, summer jumper. I picked the insert up and tried to discreetly jam it back into my wallet, but Chinedu grabbed it and stared at the image.

"I know him."

"He used to play professional football—" I said.

"Chuck," he said.

"Ya . . ."

"I know him."

"How?

We moved towards the front of the food line.

"I worked at the golf course where he golfed this summer. Me, Chuck, and Graham. We were tight, we're buddies."

"What?"

"Ya, ya," he said. Then he stopped for a moment, laughing.

"This is crazy, J. So crazy," Chinedu said. Chinedu's wide smile exuded an electric charm. "He told me about you."

"What?!"

Chinedu looked at me and shook his head in disbelief as he handed the photo insert back to me. "Ya, ya. He told me and Graham about you."

He leaned into the food counter and placed his order with the woman in the hairnet who was serving up a meal of chicken, steamed vegetables, and rice. I stood there, wide-eyed, mouth agape. The woman assembled Chinedu's food on a white plate and placed it on top of his brown, plastic tray.

"He told me he had a daughter—a good girl, a pretty girl," Chinedu said with a wink. "He told me to look out for you and I said, oh ya? Pretty girl? Ya, ya, ya, me and Graham. Ya, we'll look out for her."

He winked and then squeezed me around the shoulders before letting go to slide his tray off the counter. He headed towards the dining hall, but I stood there and stared down at that photo for some time.

A few days before I left for school in the summer of 1999, my father mentioned to me that while he was golfing earlier that summer he had met two guys who were in their upper years at the same university I was going to. He had forgotten to tell me at the time, but he wanted to tell me about it, because they promised to help me get adjusted. They were nice guys, he said. They played on one of the varsity teams at school (he couldn't remember what sport). When he told me for the second time that they were black, as though that would be my ticket to finding them, I started shaking my head before he finished, fearing the inevitable. *Please tell me, you didn't.*

He told me that while he was waiting for a cart one day, he told them he had a daughter who would be starting there that fall.

Just tell me you didn't.

He told them I was a soccer player, that I was living in the all-girls residence, that I wasn't shy. She's taking *drama*, he would have said. He would have made the face he makes whenever he speaks about my interest in the arts—the eyebrow raise and the eye roll that denotes the flaky, flighty nature he believes is inherent in artists.

Just tell me you didn't . . .

He told them my name but he couldn't remember their names. He told them they should try to find me. This is when I audibly moaned with loud, dramatic emphasis.

"Daaaaaad!"

"What?"

"How could you do that?"

"Do what? They're good guys. They seemed like good guys."

I shook my head, because my father never understood me.

The thing that strikes me now about how I met Chinedu is not the providential part of our beginning; it's not the seeming coincidence of Chinedu forgetting about my father's request and befriending me that first day on instinct. It's not that, although that's interesting. It's that my father gave me what I needed before I knew what I was looking for—black friends who had diverse backgrounds but common goals, who could connect with people from different races, who would help me form a better understanding of what it meant to be black in Canada.

12

L IFE in Canada, in the suburbs of Toronto where I grew up, is different than it is in Toledo. I couldn't explain just what the differences were until recently, but I felt it even when I was little.

My grandma Earline lived in the east end of Toledo in a brown, brick, single-storey seniors facility that was surrounded by a dried-up cornfield. The building was hot and the carpets were murky shades of orange; the hallways reeked of mothballs. Only what I remember most about going to my grandmother's apartment had nothing to do with the aesthetics of her building. It's what I noticed when we crossed an important intersection that divided the east end from the west end of Toledo.

The west end, where my grandma Dorothy lived and where we stayed when we visited, looked like blue-collar towns I had seen in Ontario—ordinary people of various races from a spectrum of lower, middle, and upper classes. On the way to my grandma Earline's we would pass the university—a vibrant student community bustling with activity. We would also drive by a neighbourhood of large houses with charming shutters and flagstone walkways, home to Toledo's wealthiest white people. I remember wondering why rich, white Americans put iron statues of black boys in jockey outfits next to their gardens.

Past the intersection of Dorr Street and Secor Road, the atmosphere changed quite vividly. Everyone in the east end of Toledo was black. On the streets and in the stores, on the buses and in the playgrounds, there was a different feeling—a heaviness that was palpable. I saw women dressed in large grey sweatshirts, faded blue jeans, and white running shoes shuffling sluggishly along the sidewalks. Others leaned against bus stop poles, arms crossed, faces indignant. Old women pushed grocery carts, mouths chewing gum, skin thin and wrinkled like tissue paper. Black men with backs that curved like aged trees sat in rocking chairs or on the stoops of their houses. Young men in bright clothes and torn jeans wore gold chains that clanked and jingled; they stood next to young women who were wearing T-shirts that stretched over round bellies. They all seemed to move, subtle and slow, like puddles in a heat wave.

Whenever we visited Grandma Earline, I brought a book with me. When we reached the east end I buried myself in the pages to avoid making eye contact with the people on the other side of the window. I didn't understand why until recently.

There were two Food Town grocery stores in Toledo that we frequented whenever we visited my grandmothers—one on either side of the city. My siblings and I named them White Food Town and Black Food Town based on the location.

The parking lot at White Food Town on the west side of the city was paved smooth-straight white stripes on fresh, black asphalt. The inside of the store was always clean and scented with baked goods and fresh bread. The lights were bright and shone in a way that made everything feel light and cool like lemonade.

The parking lot at Black Food Town, in the east end, had crumbling and cracked craters; it had a large section where beer was sold in forty-ounce bottles. Women in the east end shopped in hair rollers, robes, and slippers. Black boys in big shirts and heavy pants posed outside the doors, which slid open, slow and squeaky. I never saw a white person in Black Food Town.

"Was that there before?" Damon said one day, when I was eleven, as we stood in front of White Food Town, eyes looking up at the sign on the front lawn—black, capital, plastic letters on dirty, white, individual rectangles.

Skye shrugged. "I think so. Maybe?"

In diagonal letters that angled up and overlapped the "N" in Food Town was an addition to the sign—four cursive letters overtop part of the main logo, which didn't appear on the sign at Black Food Town: *P-l-u-s*. White Food Town was officially called Food Town *Plus*. We thought this was hilarious and pointed it out to my mother, but she didn't say anything. So we told our father when we got back to my grandma Dorothy's apartment. He was watching college football in the den.

"*That's* why it's so clean," I told him through laughter. "When white people shop at a store, they call it 'Plus'!"

My father clicked his tongue on the roof of his mouth, huffed in disapproval. It was the same way he responded years later, when I asked him why my grandmother hadn't stayed in school, the same way he reacted when I told him I didn't believe people still used the "N" word. A mixture of concern and disappointment, as though I just didn't get it. Which shouldn't have surprised him.

When I asked Don Fair what life was like in Toledo back in the sixties in the months following Dr. King's assassination, he sighed into the receiver. As he spoke there was a change in his voice, a soft, slowness that was careful and thought-filled. Although part of me wondered what a white guy from Canton, Ohio, understood about the race war of the sixties.

"The first football game, the freshmen, we had to be ushers," Don said. "While we were working, we could see it—at Dorr

Street—we could see fires. The skies were orange. Probably less than a mile away, the skies were orange. Fires, fires burning, you know."

"From what? Why?"

There was silence on the other end of the line for a moment.

"You know not being right there, I don't know who set the fires, what was being burnt, but you could see areas of the town that were—the sky was orange."

By the time the first football game was over and the fans had all dispersed, the fires he'd seen in the east end had dulled to embers. After the game, Don headed towards a drugstore across campus with a white teammate named Paul Highman. It was the week before classes would start for the semester and the campus streets were quiet, the buildings dark, their way lit by lampposts that lined the pedestrian pathways.

A car drove towards the pair, headlights bright. It slowed as it passed, then squealed into reverse, before stopping next to them. The four doors to the car opened and five men, all black, stepped out and surrounded them. They struck Don in the jaw, then Paul. They threw punches that landed on the pair again and again and again. Paul must have managed to writhe away from the scuffle, because at some point Don was alone, surrounded. The group of men punched him until he struggled out of their reach and sprinted down a hill in his moccasins. They ran after him, but Don was fast; he didn't look back or stop running even when a rock hit him.

When he reached a tall, chain-link fence, Don climbed up as his attackers gripped the fence, panting with exhaustion. The men looked back at their car—several metres away, lights on, doors wide open, as Don leaped down on the other side. Don disappeared into the darkness, as the men turned and headed back to their vehicle. Don arrived at Carter Hall as Paul and a few other teammates, who'd heard about the ambush, were pouring out of the residence. Don spent the first six weeks of classes drinking his meals from a straw.

As Don told the story, there was no hint of bitterness or accusation or resentment in his voice. I only sensed his own remorse and regret over the way things were back then and the position he found himself in—a position he hadn't fully understood before he arrived at university.

"That was literally an offshoot of what was going on—the riots and all that. I literally got a first-hand taste of it my first week at the University of Toledo."

I thought about those men from Toledo's east end and the violence that erupted that night for a long time after I spoke with Don Fair. I thought about my own frustrations, about the different ways people responded to what was going on back then in America.

The 1968 Olympics in Mexico City came on the heels of the death of Dr. King and the riots that followed. John Carlos, who qualified to represent America in the 200-metre dash, wanted to boycott the games as a way of speaking out against racial injustice. However, many of America's black Olympians were unwilling to participate. The International Olympic Committee warned all of the participants that political demonstrations of any kind would not be tolerated.

In the finals for the 200 metres, John Carlos finished third. Fellow American Tommie Smith set a new world record when he finished ahead of Australia's silver medallist. At the medal ceremony, as the American flag rose in tandem amidst the sounds of the epic "Star-Spangled Banner," the Afro-wearing teammates bowed their heads solemnly. Smith raised his gloved right hand in a fist, Carlos his gloved left—a demonstration of black unity. As onlookers in the stadium booed incessantly, a photographer captured the moment. The picture made front-page news around the world.

Some said the gesture was powerful, noble. Others considered it un-American. On the cover of a special Olympic issue, *Time* magazine displayed an image of the five-ring Olympic logo; the 1968 motto "Faster, Higher, Stronger" was replaced with the epithetical words "Angrier, Nastier, Uglier." The International Olympic Committee banned them from the games permanently.

I remember seeing the poster of those two black men and the famous image of their raised fists when I was younger. I knew what the picture was about in the vague way I *knew* about impor-tant things I saw in passing back then. When I learned that the Olympics took place the year my father and Don Fair started college at the University of Toledo, a few weeks after the fires on Dorr Street, I thought about those two athletes and the words on the *Time* cover quite differently. I thought about how angry and ugly I felt when I spoke out to people who wronged me.

Leah Gillingham and I became known as Black Lightning on the University of Guelph women's soccer team. We were fast and flew down the field in similar, torrential attack mode. By my second year of varsity soccer, two more black girls had joined the roster—two girls who were just as fast and demonstrated the same kind of athleticism. There was Jenny, who was from the suburbs of Toronto, and Natalie, who came from out East. Jenny had milky-brown skin and big, curly hair that she held down with elastics like Leah and I did. Natalie had caramel skin and straight, light brown, honey-hinted hair.

People didn't always know Natalie was black, but I saw it immediately, because my mother had taught me how to tell when someone has even just a little bit of black in them. It's in the kink of their hair and the tan of their skin; it's in the way they turn that extra bit of brown when the sun beats down on them. Leah, Jenny, and Natalie each had one black parent, but we all became known as Black Lightning. While we weren't always the fanciest players, we could make up the difference with sheer quickness.

We were grouped together once in an exercise that tested speed and passing, and we won handily. When we sat down on the grass to stretch after practice, we laughed about the dominance of Black Lightning in front of our teammates—brunettes and red-heads and blondes from cities and small towns across Canada.

Our coach was blonde with a short boy haircut, and her family was British. She had fair skin that blotched red in the sunlight. She dressed in the tracksuits and T-shirts that marked her soccer career milestones, and watched European football league every Saturday with her goalkeeper husband.

As the girls on the team continued to discuss the results of the exercise, and as Leah boasted about our performance exuberantly, I chimed in that Black Lightning was unbeatable. The other girls laughed and fired back that next time they would beat us. When I said that was impossible, that we had superior black genetics, our coach interrupted.

"Let's be honest, none of you are *really* black," she said.

I looked at Leah, Jenny, and Natalie, but none of them seemed bothered. Leah just laughed and said our coach was just jealous. But as the laughter trailed off and the moment started to pass, I felt something inside me rising; I felt something that I could not convince to stay silent even when the team gathered their belongings to head back to the team room. I walked towards my coach, my heart sprinting.

"Just to be clear, I'm really black," I told her.

My coach looked up from her clipboard, her tone splitting my words with scepticism. "Well . . ."

"Well, what?" I said.

She tilted her head side to side, but said nothing.

"How would you feel if someone told you that you that you weren't really white or really British?" I stepped closer to her, the grey metal part of her clipboard grazing the front of my sweat-soaked T-shirt. "I don't care what they consider themselves, but I'm black. Don't question it again."

I walked off the field, but I didn't feel better. Not even a little bit. I felt wild and out of control, like a bucking bronco trying to shake off a rider who's steadfast and stubborn, frantically kicking, hooves landing on nothing. I had lost my temper, but what was worse, I knew it was futile. I would go back to the team room to calm myself down while they wondered what had gotten into me, why I was so defensive. They would wonder what the big deal was. That thought made me feel angrier and uglier than ever.

At the University of Guelph, I learned a lot about twentieth-century America that would help me understand why the east end of Toledo made me so uncomfortable. After centuries of slavery, American history had become deeply rooted in America's geography—generations of men and women with limited means and education living with little, generation after generation, unable to rise above their circumstances given the obstacles of their environment.

When I drove through the east end when I was younger, I didn't understand it, and by the time I got to high school, I had started to do what my father did so often—I started to downplay what I saw there. When I understood the struggles and the ongoing trials of Black America, it became important to me to understand that history. It became important for me not to hide when I was wronged or angry, but to wrestle with the origin. I needed to redefine what it meant for me to be black, and I needed to be able to explain why that definition was so important.

I started to watch black films and read novels that intentionally explored black stories. I paid attention to shows and plays and interviews with men and women who could teach me about black culture. I gathered history anthologies and read about the wide array of black history makers—ordinary people, political leaders, writers, and athletes. In the collection of stories I watched and read, my heroes came to be revolutionaries—people like Mohammad Ali, John Carlos, and Tommie Smith. They were intense activists who had faced oppression and adversity; they had risen from tragedy and subjugation by raising radical flags of resistance.

My favourite movie was a film about the founding of the Black Panther Party for Self-Defense. I bought the soundtrack for the film and listened to the passionate, dark, hip-hop, and the richly spoken poetry in the privacy of my bedroom. I listened to black voices talking black and repeated the words with fervent unanimity. So when my father told me that he had actually seen the Black Panther Party march down the streets of Toledo, my eyes grew wide with excitement.

In the late sixties, Huey Newton and Bobby Seale were dissatisfied with the progress of the peace marches and the non-violent approach of other civil rights activists. They started the Black Panther Party to protect black Americans who were experiencing unjust treatment and encountering police brutality. Followers of the Black Panther Party carried loaded shotguns publicly, affirming their constitutional right to bear unconcealed arms; they wore black leather coats with military-style hats and carried tape recorders, law books, and cameras to challenge and record encounters with law enforcement. They held protests

(above)

My mother and Grandpa Harry Dennis on Searles Road, 1958

(left)

My father and his brother Bryant, 1970

My father and Grandma Earline, 1973

Holy Redeemer football team, 1962

Notre Dame High School, 1965

Studying in Carter Hall East, 1969

University of Toledo, 1972

My father and coach Frank Lauterbur, 1970

Great-Grandma
Ethel Walker,
Grandma
Dorothy Dennis,
my mother,
Grandma Earline
Ealey, 1972

My family, 1981

Damon and my father, 1993

Hamilton Tiger-Cats, 1972

CHUCK EALEY

Mark and me, 2008

Visiting Charles Ealey Sr.'s gravesite

Visiting Portsmouth flood wall

Visiting Municipal Stadium

and marches where they raised their fists and shouted "Black Power"—a phrase that caught on quickly among a growing faction of educated, young blacks from northern cities who were hungry for equality.

My father stumbled on the Toledo chapter of the Black Panther Party when he was on his way to a get-together at the house of one of his teammates during his first semester in 1968. He was walking down the sidewalk towards the east end of the city, when he noticed a crowd heading towards him.

"I went down to Dorr Street," my father told me, "and there were the Black Panthers marching down the street with guns. Forty of them. I was shocked. It was okay to have unconcealed weapons out."

I pictured my father in his navy varsity coat with the felt yellow T, a small basket-weave toque over a small Afro, tight turtleneck, bell-bottoms—a group clad in black marching towards him. Their large Afros, dark sunglasses, black berets, handguns, and shotguns held in front of them, military style, bullet casings draped across their chests like pageant sashes. The heavy sound of synchronized stomp thundered inside me.

"What did you do?"

My father pulled his head back abruptly, looked at me, his mouth tight, his eyebrows furrowed, puzzled by the question.

"I went back to campus," he said. "I wanted to get out of there as soon as possible."

I nodded at my father, but inside, my stomach sagged with disappointment. I wanted my father to tell me that he walked right out there and marched with the Panthers, that he bought a black jacket that day, that he raised his fist, that he said Black Power. At the very least, I wanted to know that he watched those men march with some measure of admiration, and had some urge to take up arms in the war for civil rights and equality. I wanted this to be one of those Dreamland sit-in moments. But my father just went back to campus.

I remember reading about American soldiers battling Desert Storm, trapped POWs featured in photos on the cover of the daily newspaper, bloody, tortured, and beaten. Members of the Canadian military, however, were often pictured shovelling cities and towns out of snowstorms. They were covered performing special efforts in disadvantaged countries. It's probably because, in general, Canadians are pacifists—humanitarian, peacekeepers. Despite his American upbringing, my father has always been very passive about all that's happened to him—willing to shuffle off troubles and hardships and let them melt away under the warmth of opportunity.

While I'm a peacekeeper, a humanitarian who shies away from discord, black history is the one thing that makes me feel like a fiery rebel. When I discover wrongdoing, injustice or suffering, it's the one thing that makes me want to march down the road, fist held high like a Panther.

13

M Y FATHER SAYS he doesn't keep secrets, but when I was younger, he and I maintained an elusiveness of sharing that meant we lost all kinds of stories in the verbal economy of our conversations. Our talks were sporadic, taking place between school and practices, my father's business meetings and social events. They were marred by an efficiency that hinged on two main criteria: 1) say only what's necessary; 2) avoid conflict by anticipating it.

This is how conversations typically unfolded on a Saturday when my father came home and I was on my way somewhere:

Dad: Where are you going?

Me: Out.

Dad: (*exhibiting facial signs of disapproval*) With who?

Me: Friends.

Dad: (*sighing*) Which friends?

Me: (*sighing back*) You don't know them. (*He waits. I pause, roll my eyes with resignation.*) Chris.

Dad: Chris who?

Me: Exactly.

Then out the door I would go, letting the door slam behind me, because: a) if he really cared, he would know who Chris was; b) I had nothing else to say; and c) slamming doors killed the awkward silences that followed these encounters.

It wasn't until I discovered how much I didn't know about him and how much I wanted to know about history, that I realized how much I lost by maintaining our broken interactions, how much I misunderstood his silences.

I thought my father kept secrets because he was hiding things or trying to protect me. It turns out my father's biggest "secrets" were the stories of his darkest and most difficult struggles.

When I was growing up and I asked my father who the boy was in the framed picture in my grandmother's apartment, he would just say, "That's my brother, Bryant."

Only he didn't elaborate. And I don't have any uncles.

The boy in the picture had light brown skin and dark eyes; he was smiling gently and wore a T-shirt with thick orange and white stripes. The tone of my father's voice implied he would rather not talk about it—this line of questioning was not one he approved of. Now I recognize that tone as the mark of a story of great importance. I know to press harder. I know not to let up, even when there's resistance.

So when we sat on the couches in the family room, next to the orange glow of the fireplace, and I brought up Bryant Spaulding, I asked my father for everything he could remember, even the broken bits of memory—the parts he knew for certain and the parts he heard from my grandmother. I asked him to tell me, from the beginning, about what happened to Bryant.

On a warm fall day in 1968, my grandmother folds clothes on her lap—a pile of small T-shirts, tiny shorts, a pair of blue socks with small embroidered yellow sailboats; her sister Alberta hangs wet cotton sheets nearby on a clothesline. There's a chill in the wind that's refreshing in the sunshine.

Bryant throws a small ball in the air, watches it fly, then runs after it. He waddles across the yard in the North End complex as the two women speak across their baskets of dishevelled laundry.

"How's Junior?"

"Good. He's doin' good up there. Real good," my grandmother says, but her heart aches and twists and her eyes start to water.

Bryant throws the ball, chases it and laughs, cheeks flushed from running. "Look, Mummy."

"Good job, baby," she says.

My grandmother places her folded clothes in a basket as Alberta continues to stretch out wrinkles in the panel of fabric.

"George been by?" Alberta says.

My grandmother shakes her head and grabs a stained shirt from another basket. She walks over to the rumbling washer and Bryant rushes to catch up to her, arm looping around her thigh, head leaned against her. She slides the shirt toward the rollers of the washer and rubs Bryant's head.

"You wash da clothes, Mummy?"

She nods and heads back to her chair, while Bryant leans against the machine and lets it hum against his body. And when the stained shirt starts to bunch, Bryant watches as the machine lets out a low murmur of discomfort.

Fingers gripped around the basin, Bryant reaches forward to stretch out the cloth, to ease it through the way his mother and aunt did so often—one hand on the cloth, the other hand further up towards the bunching. He keeps reaching, stretching his fingers further out, ear pressed against the basin. And when my grandmother looks up, just a moment too late, she calls out for her son as the washing machine starts up again, as it rolls its jaws around the boy's hand tightly. Bryant opens his mouth and inhales as tears puddle and race downward. He exhales a shrill wail as Alberta rushes over and lifts the lever to release the pressure, my grandmother holding Bryant closely.

Shhhh, Bryant. *Shhhh*, she says, rocking her son against her.

Alberta places something cold over his hand, now a reddish-purple, but Bryant only screams louder. *Shhh. Shhh. Shhh.* And with a nod from her sister, my grandmother packs Bryant up to take her son to the doctor.

———————————

"In the North End, people didn't go to the doctors too often," my father told me. "There was a sort of stigma."

What the stigma was wasn't clear to me, or even to my father. It probably had something to do with white men in white coats with trays of sharp silver objects and vials of funny-flavoured liquids.

The injury to Bryant's hand healed within weeks, but a series of persistent fevers followed. Doctors initially attributed the fevers to some kind of infection or to Bryant's obesity. But when unusual pockets of swelling persistently developed, my grandmother went back to the doctors in search of answers. Perhaps after all those years cleaning hospitals, my grandmother recognized something she had seen in other patients.

After months of fevers and swelling and tests, blood tests revealed that Bryant Spaulding had a low white blood cell count. In the winter of 1969, when my father was finishing his first year of university, Bryant was diagnosed with a form of cancer known as lymphoma. My grandmother was told he wouldn't make it to Christmas. Cancer was invading his immune system.

So my grandmother packed her bags and moved to Dayton, Ohio, where there was a children's hospital where Bryant would undergo treatment. It was also closer to Toledo, which meant my father could visit more easily.

As my grandmother and Bryant relocated, America was undergoing a different kind of transition. Richard Milhous Nixon was given control of the country; he promised the country a change of course and new beginnings.

Each moment in history is a fleeting time, precious and unique. But some stand out as moments of beginning, in which courses are set that shape decades or centuries. This can be such a moment.

History would prove Nixon's future in politics "fleeting" as a result of his own poor judgment, but 1969 did mark the start of a course-shaping history for my father. It was the year my father's Rocket stardom started to take flight.

14

I REMEMER WALKING into the University of Toledo's Glass Bowl Stadium when I was sixteen to watch a homecoming game. I walked down the rows of steel silver bleachers and across to the seat on my ticket. I sat down and looked up to see a massive mural on the side of one of the stadium buildings. The mural featured a man in a Rockets jersey holding a football. I remember staring at that young man for some time before I read the text at the bottom and realized it was my father.

In accordance with National Collegiate Athletic Association (NCAA) regulations, varsity freshmen on college football teams were "red-shirted" for their first year. They were not permitted to compete formally against other colleges until their sophomore year of college. They practised with the varsity, learned the plays, did the drills, but they watched every matchup as freshmen from the sidelines.

"Our main thing was to survive and get through those first three months as cannon fodder for the varsity," Don said. "They went through a lot of guys. It was pretty standard operating procedure back then. There were all-state guys and really good athletes who weren't mentally tough enough and they ran them off. They didn't care. Those of us who were able to persevere, it made us closer, and when we started to compete it made us tougher."

My father and Don Fair got their first opportunity to compete for starting positions at spring training camp in 1969— two weeks of intensive conditioning, drills, and scrimmages that determined positions for the fall. The starting quarterback at the time was a junior named Steve Jones. He had one year left, but at spring camp Jones struggled. He dropped snaps and threw passes that barely reached receivers. He fumbled and threw interceptions, while my father completed passes and played with incredible precision.

On the final day of camp, as the players warmed up for the Old-timers Game—a game that pitted new players against the veterans who were on the verge of graduation—Coach Lauterbur pulled my father aside to talk to him.

"Chuck, I know you had a good spring practice, but Steve's the senior quarterback. We're going to start him," Lauterbur said.

"Did that bother you?" I asked my father.

"That's just how Frank was," my father said with a shrug. "I figured I would get my chance eventually."

Eventually came sooner than even my father anticipated. By halftime at the Old-timers Game the younger Rockets were down 14–3.

"Warm up. You're starting the second half," Coach Lauterbur said to my father.

My father stepped out onto the field and huddled the offence together to start the third quarter. He clapped them into position, then stood behind the centre, hands steady as he scanned the defence. My father ran the ball, scrambled, and stayed in the pocket; he threw long balls and short ones, quick passes, and executed well-timed hand-offs. He led the team from an eleven-point deficit to victory. After the game, Coach Lauterbur told my father that when they returned to camp in August, my father would be the starting quarterback.

"That's how it worked. That's how I ended up winning the starting position," my father told me.

"Were you nervous going into that game?" I asked.

"I never really thought about it. I just said, Okay, let's go, let's see where it all comes out. And it worked out okay."

I shook my head with bemusement. My father is still under the impression that what happened to him was ordinary. For most of my life I believed him. Until I found a book of newspaper articles from *The Blade*, Toledo's local paper from 1971. Inside the book were accounts of every game my father played as a Rocket, starting with the first time he formally took the field as the University of Toledo's starting quarterback.

The Blade
September 21, 1969

ROCKETS FLY HIGH IN OPENER, 45–18
Jim Taylor

The swift, young Rockets scored the first time they handled the ball, putting over a touchdown after just 1:24 had been played.

And they were to repeat five more times before the game ended.

After another win, against Marshall University, my father faced the conference's strongest opponent—defending Mid-American Conference champions Ohio University. They were led by one of the coaches who had refused to offer my father a scholarship at quarterback back when he was at Notre Dame High School.

"Ohio University had gone to the Peach Bowl," Don Fair told me. "They played Georgia and the game ended in a 45–45 tie. They had an All-Conference quarterback. He and Todd Schneider were a record-setting quarterback-receiver combination. And they had everybody back for another year. They were picked overwhelmingly to win the conference and here we were, this upstart group of sophomores. That was the game where your dad and I began our connection. That was a big moment."

The Blade
October 5, 1969

ROCKETS IN ORBIT, BELT BOBCATS, 34–9

University of Toledo's mercurial Mod Squad destroyed the establishment Saturday night before 19,223 howling witnesses in the Glass Bowl. And there wasn't a growl of protest as the Rockets belted proud defending Mid-American Conference champion Ohio University 34–9, in a show that was as stunning as it was one-sided. Rocket sophomores Chuck Ealey and Al Baker, Steve Schnitkey and John Niezgoda, Mel Long and Don Fair led this charge that snapped the chains Ohio had wrapped around the MAC [Mid-American Conference] for two years.[2]

In their fourth game, the Rockets faced Bowling Green University—Toledo's arch nemesis. In the book of articles, there were two full pages of editorials, articles, and play-by-play accounts, dedicated to the one game, all of which centred on the fierce matchup and the bizarre windstorm that rolled through BGU's Doyt L. Perry Stadium in front of a record crowd of nearly 21,000.

Behind at the half, Bowling Green charged back in the 3rd and 4th quarters. With less than a minute left in the game, Bowling Green pulled ahead 26–24. The BGU fans cheered hysterically. My father took the field with forty-nine seconds on the clock, sixty-eight yards from the end zone. Bowling Green fans continued to scream and rose to their feet, prepared for victory.

The Blade
November 21, 2000

THE WIN IN THE WIND
[looking back to October 12, 1969]

First off, there was the wind. Whipping like a son of a gun, darn near howling as it caromed between the stands ...

"I remember Chuck telling everybody that we had 49 seconds," field goal kicker Ken Crots said in a post-game interview, "that we had to give it all we had left and make something happen."

My father completed two passes to Don Fair to bring the team within forty yards of the end zone. They were down by two with two seconds left on the clock. The Rockets called on Ken Crots.

Two of Crots's kicks had been blocked that day already. A third had blown just wide of the uprights. Bowling Green fans hoped for one more foul-up; they prayed for the wind to blow fiercely as Crots lined himself up on the thirty-seven yard line.

Ken Crots, for all the marbles.

Crots stepped back and eyed the ball as the flags on the tops of the uprights flapped frantically. As Crots approached the ball at a run, something happened to the wind, something everyone noticed as those flags slowed, then rested.

It stopped in its tracks. A split second of calm.

In that brief stillness, Crots struck the ball. All of the fans in the stadium watched in an eerie moment of silence. The ball flipped towards the uprights. A young boy standing under the posts raised both hands emphatically.

"What I remember most is the kid raising his arms up. That's when I knew it was good," Coach Lauterbur said in an interview.

Speaking of his Bowling Green players, Coach Don Nehlen said, "I've never seen kids cry like that."

To fans in Toledo, the game was amazing—the results and the miraculous halting of the wind for Crots's kick like Moses parting the Red Sea for the Israelites.

What amazes me about the Bowling Green game and the rest of the wins from my father's undefeated sophomore season though has little to do with the victories. It's what my father was doing after each game, between each successful finish. He didn't celebrate with his teammates or go to parties. My father got in his car and drove five hours to Dayton to visit with his mother and his ailing four-year-old brother, always returning in time for classes and practices.

No one—not his teammates, his coaches, or even his friends—knew about Bryant's condition.

When I turned seventeen, I developed a rare infection. When the pain became overwhelming, I went to the hospital where I was scheduled for emergency surgery. A doctor was brought in to remove a section of my intestine—a procedure and occasion so rare for a person of my age, it was written up in a medical journal. I spent the week after surgery in the hospital, slowly reintroducing liquids and solids into my diet as a tube in my nose sucked green bile from my belly and dumped it in a clear bucket by my bedside. My father stopped by most days, albeit briefly.

"How are you doing, Boo?" he would say, as he moved around the hospital room. He would check the charts, the view from the window, look at what I was watching on television.

"Fine, Dad. Better," I would say as I watched him.

Eventually, he would wander off in search of something or someone—a doctor to answer his questions, a nurse to give him updates. When he finally did find someone, he would ask *them* how I was doing. As though I hadn't told him. They would tell him I was doing well and I would sigh with a look that said, I told you so. I would tell him to go to work, because I could tell he was in a rush—there was work at the office, and being with me was putting him behind schedule. He couldn't sit still for a moment.

"I'm okay, really. Damon is going to sit with me and watch reruns of *Law and Order*. Mom will be by soon. It's okay. Really. You can go now," I would say to reassure him.

Now I see that time I spent recovering in the hospital very differently. Now I think about my father driving alone on Interstate 75 in 1969, the dull glow of white lights enveloping his car as it moved through the darkness. I think about him walking into a room where his four-year-old brother rested with little hope of recovery. A boy who wanted his big brother there with him every second.

Those hospital visits when my father stopped by and saw my face grey with pain, my eyes dark and sunken, must have been so difficult. He must have been so worried. I wish he had told me about Bryant earlier. I wish I had understood the signs of my father's devotion.

15

I WAS RECENTLY ASKED what I remember most about my father from my childhood. I thought about the way he called me Booper or Boo when I was younger. Or the way he terrified my friends with his stoicism. I thought of how frightened I felt when my mother would say, "Your father is coming to your game tonight."

In the end, I chose something that was a constant, everyday thing, something I thought everyone should know about him.

"I always remember him loving my mother," I told them.

There's something about the way my father treated my mother that always made me feel secure, even during my father's unsettling silences. There were gifts, cards, trips, special nights out, and occasional compliments.

When everything else in my relationship with my father seemed tenuous or volatile, when his absences left me wanting, my parents were the ideal of love and stability. Only when my father started to tell me about this part of his life, how he met my mother, I discovered that it wasn't entirely true. It only started like a fairy tale.

My father grips the steering wheel of his car with his right hand, left arm on the door of his black convertible in the fall of 1969. John Saunders taps his fingers to Earth, Wind and Fire, dancing in September on the radio. A girl in the backseat holds a backpack tightly against her, her hair swirling loosely as the wind blows around them. Tall trees stretch towards the sky, their long, limber branches hanging over a quiet neighbourhood in West Toledo as red and gold leaves fall like feathers.

"Here. You can stop here," she says.

The two men look at one another and laugh, and the girl leans forward between the seats, placing her hand on the driver's shoulder.

"Chuck, stop here," she says, her voice straining slightly. "Right here."

"Saundo, she wants me to stop," my father says to his friend, their smiles full of mocking.

"I hear you, brother," says Saunders. "But I just don't feel right leaving this fine-looking lady out here on the mean and dangerous streets of Toledo." When Saunders turns around to see the young girl's expression, her eyes pleading and fearful, he laughs even harder. "We're gentlemen, after all," he says, through laughter.

"John, *please*," she whispers.

"Hear that, Chuck? Josephine said please!"

Josephine puts her head down and slides herself lower in the seat as the car continues slowly forward, the two men laughing hysterically.

Josephine West, a senior at Rogers High School, wasn't allowed to date college boys because her parents said they were trouble. She told her parents she was studying with a friend so she could spend time with her boyfriend John Saunders, a sophomore on the University of Toledo football squad. When my father offered to drive her home, Josephine made him promise to stop a few blocks away to preserve the lie of her story. She waited until the car stopped before she raised her head and peeked over the lowered window. When she saw a white house with red shutters, she breathed a sigh of relief. She was a few blocks away from the home where her parents were expecting her.

Maybe Josephine kissed Saunders on the cheek; maybe she stormed away, unforgiving and angry at the boys for their teasing; maybe she tapped gently on the hood to thank my father for the drive, grateful despite the comic cruelty. My father doesn't remember that part of the story. What he does remember about that moment is a girl in wide-bottomed jeans standing at the door of the white house with the red shutters on it. He remembers seeing her search through a backpack for her keys, and lift them towards the doorknob. He remembers watching her step inside the house and look around, before closing the door behind her, as my father nudged John Saunders.

"You see that girl, Saundo?" he said to his teammate.

Saunders nodded. "What about her?"

"I'm going to marry that girl," my father told him.

A few weeks later, my mother closed the front door inside another West Toledo home as an older couple, the Gandys, made their way down their front walkway for a special evening. Dr. Gandy was the University of Toledo football team's doctor, and a few weeks before the end of the season, he and his wife called on their family babysitter to watch their daughter while they attended a function. Their son was at a friend's house and their daughter Robyn was asleep by the time my mother stepped into the foyer and sat down at a round coffee table covered in University of Toledo football magazines.

She spread them out and picked up the most recent edition. She skimmed through the pages, pausing at the athletes' photos. She ran her finger across the glossy black-and-white photographs. *Pete Alsup, Ron Bailey.* She was looking for freshmen or sophomores. Handsome. Black. Distinguished. *Al Baker. Don Bell.* Mature college boys, she thought, as she continued to turn the pages.

Chuck Ealey.

She traced the information with her finger: *Chuck Ealey, QB, Sophomore, Hometown: Portsmouth, Ohio.* His eyes were serious, intent, and deep, and she tilted her head and stared, ran her finger around the image, smiling quietly. *That's him.* She leaned back, the magazine resting across her lap as her fingers tapped the face of the young stranger. *I'm going to marry him.*

"We met at a basketball game," my mother said. She held onto a cup of coffee and I watched as steam rose off the surface. "Your father was getting an award, I think. I asked the Gandys about him and they arranged for us to meet. They brought me to the game and Butch Gandy introduced us. Butch knew all the ballplayers."

My mother took a sip of her coffee.

I asked her what she saw in my father back then, what stood out in that picture. With her white mug close to her lips, she smiled, took a sip, and then placed the mug with the blue, stencilled flower on it on the table.

"He was nice. Polite," she said.

I leaned over and waved my hands to encourage her to share more details. I wanted to know what he looked like, what she thought of him when he stood in front of her. I wanted to know how his eyes changed, the moment he recognized the girl from the white house with the red shutters. I wanted to know what they both saw before they even met that made them certain of a marriage-calibre connection.

"He was wearing his letterman jacket," she finally said.

My mother leaned back, one hand wrapped around the mug, the other cupped gently beneath it. I could tell by the way she turned and looked through the sliding door, the way she lifted her mug and sipped slowly, that she remembered the moment distinctly. I could tell that she remembered what she felt forty years ago.

"And then what?"

She placed the mug on the table and leaned over it, watching the surface, and then looked up with a mischievous grin. She shrugged facetiously.

"I started to pay attention to football."

The Blade
November 23, 1969

TU BLANKS XAVIER, FINISHES PERFECT
Jim Taylor

I am curious (fellow). Who is No. I in the state of Ohio?

University of Toledo swarmed over Xavier University 35–0 Saturday afternoon to finish the first unbeaten, untied football season in the school's history.

And while the Rockets were pumping methodically along toward their 10th straight victory, Ohio State's reputation as a super team was crumbling in Ann Arbor, Michigan.

[. . .] Sophomore Chuck Ealey, throwing for two touchdowns and running 34 yards for another, triggered the third-period explosion.

My mother remembers learning through her father, who followed Rockets football, that the University of Toledo quarterback Butch Gandy introduced her to at the basketball game had quarterbacked a team that had won every game that season. The Rockets were the new Mid-American Conference champions; they would be playing in the Tangerine Bowl in Florida just after Christmas. The team would leave for Orlando a few days before the game to get used to the warm temperatures.

My mother sent two cards to Florida with Dr. Gandy that December, addressed to the team's starting quarterback. *Merry Christmas*, one said. The other: *I look forward to seeing you when you get back.* They were signed in loopy cursive: *Sherri Kay Dennis.*

My father thought it was a nice gesture, but he was focused on the bowl game.

The Blade
December 27, 1969

ROCKETS RIP DAVIDSON 56–33
Jim Taylor

Hurricane Toledo swept out of the North to strike this central Florida city Friday night and the tremors were felt all the way to the hills of North Carolina.

Storms like this usually are called Dolly, and Daisy, and Darlene, but Hurricane Toledo played a he-man's game in the Tangerine Bowl to destroy the gritty Davidson 56–33, before a record crowd of 16,311.

My father was named the Tangerine Bowl's Most Valuable Player, and after a visit home to see his mother and Bryant (who was doing well and had made it past the Christmas my grandmother had been dreading since receiving Bryant's dismal prognosis), he followed through with his plan. He made a call to arrange his first date with Sherri Kay Dennis in January 1970.

"We went to a frat party," my father said, with a mixture of pride and embarrassment. "Being in college and not having a lot of money, we went anywhere cheap, whether it was to a basketball game or a campus party. Most of it was college parties or campus events." He smiled, nostalgic. "No matter what though, we often ended up at Big Boy. There was one that was not too far from her house, so we would go there. I remember she would order the grilled cheese sandwich and I would always have a big hamburger."

Frisch's Big Boy is a fast-food chain we often went to as a family when Damon went to the University of Toledo. It was one of the few places that were open after night games. Rocket team members and fans went there to comfort themselves after defeat or celebrate victory. Every time my father announced the destination, my mother would cringe. Mom doesn't like Big Boy, we would tell him.

My father would wave his hand and wrinkle his face in disagreement. "Your mother loves Big Boy."

My mother frowned and rolled her eyes every time he said this.

"I never liked it. He just kept taking me there," she would tell us, hoping my father would finally get the message. "All I could order were the grilled cheese sandwiches."

I remember sitting in a booth at Big Boy after one of my brother's games sometime in the late nineties. Damon was wearing No. 16 at the University of Toledo, just like he had in high school, just like my father did. Unlike my father, however, Damon was no longer playing quarterback. In fact, because of his injuries, and his size (Damon is five foot nine; my father is three inches taller), and the level of American competition, my brother wasn't playing much of anything.

A man came over to our Big Boy booth to speak with my father. He was dressed in gold and blue, having been at the game in the Glass Bowl, where the Rockets had lost abysmally.

"Chuck, good to see you. I watched every game. Those were the days, huh?"

My father smiled politely, and signed the napkin the man placed on the table.

"I was too small to play quarterback in the States," Damon told me when I asked him about being a Rocket. "And for all four years, I was rarely in good health, physically. There was always something."

Initially, I thought my brother went to the University of Toledo for the same reasons I considered going there—because my father had connections; because it was familiar; because American scholarships meant going to school for free and that carried with it prestige and notoriety, and gave you a heightened sense of accomplishment. Now I think there was more to it. I think Damon went to the University of Toledo for the same reason we went to Portsmouth years after we both graduated from college—to understand my father, to figure out all of the things my father never shared with us.

Only when I spoke with Damon about the distance my father maintained in our family, the way I felt that my father was some-how missing or absent when I needed him, my brother disagreed adamantly.

"Dad was there. He took me places," Damon said. "I called him every day during training camp."

Without that contact, Damon told me he might not have made it through his two-a-day practices, those hot all-day summer workouts.

Maybe that's not what I meant exactly. Maybe it's not just my father's physical presence that was missing. I thought about my stint at the hospital. He was *present*, devoted even. But there's something I remembered growing up that made me feel that even when he was there, he really wasn't. Something I was trying to reconcile with the life in the North End that I now knew about—something I began to understand when I looked at his story from a different viewpoint.

My father took my mother to Dayton in the summer of 1970. She was among the few people he told about his brother. My mother remembers that my father was warm and playful with his brother, and that Bryant was active and mobile, happy, in spite of his illness.

"He had tumours in different places, but I don't remember thinking of him as being sick," my mother told me. "I remember he looked fine. He was an active four-year-old boy."

I thought of the picture that sat on my grandmother's side table—Bryant's toothy smile, round face, those eyes, glossy and round like black marbles. I thought of the four of them together—my thin, fair mother, my powerful grandmother, and those reunited brothers. I asked my mother what they were like together, how they interacted.

"Bryant was really excited to see your dad. But it wasn't like they were brothers—there was too big an age difference," my mother said. "Your father had left for school when Bryant was really young. He was more like a dad."

I thought of that sweet, chubby four-year-old boy next to my father—the Portsmouth legend, the college football star. Bryant must have hugged his brother with all his strength, and held on until he left.

"Father," for most boys, in the North End and in many of the projects in American towns and cities, meant someone who was

16

U P UNTIL RECENTLY, my ambitions in life came solely from watching my mother. I wanted to be just like her. It's one of the main reasons I was so confused for so long about whether or not I was black enough.

See, my mother is totally black but most people don't believe that. In high school, my peers always questioned it.

"You're mixed, right?" the girls at the First Table asked me one day. They had spotted my mother at one of my volleyball games.

"No. I'm black," I would quietly say.

"So your mother's mixed?" they would say.

"She's black." (This is what my mother told me to say the next-time-the-girls-at-school-want-to-know.)

"Her mother's black?"

"Yes."

"*And* her father?"

I paused before answering with rote inflection. "Her mother is black and her father is black. Her father's parents are black and mixed."

"So she's mixed."

"She's black."

"But—"

"Her great-grandfather was black and *his* wife was white. So my grandfather is three-quarters black. Which makes my mother seven-eighths black. Which makes me . . ."

They nodded with satisfaction before I finished. I could never figure out how to win that conversation. I could never figure out how to end it in a way in which everyone who was present would be certain of my blackness.

My mother's skin is the colour of ivory tusks—a hint of yellow-brown that in Canada is not nearly as definitively black as it is in America. Americans have this drop-in-the-bucket rule that's handy for people like my mother—one drop of black blood, no matter how small or seemingly invisible, makes you indisputably and *legally* African-American. It makes you part of a race with a definitive, albeit fractured, place in history.

In Canada, it's difficult to make the case that my mother is as black as my father. It doesn't look that way, and that's hard for some people. There are all these tricky subcategories in Canada that complicate things: mixed, basically white, totally black, half-breed, biracial—categories based on mathematics and classifications of blackness.

My mother has never been able to understand the measurements.

"Are you half, Mom?"

"Half of what?"

"Half white."

"No."

"But you're mixed?"

"I'm black."

"How black?"

"Just black."

"So you're black? Just black. Like black-black? Like for-sure black?"

"Yes."

"Then how come you're so light?"

"I don't know, Jael."

My mother spoke carefully in these conversations, with forced patience, and when she used my name instead of one of her nicknames for me (Matilda or Tilly), it meant her engagement in the conversation had reached its expiration point.

"How do you explain Grandpa?" I would say. "There's no way he's totally black!"

My mother wouldn't answer.

So I would stare at my grandfather's wall-mounted picture where he stood next to my grandma Dorothy, gazing at a man I hardly knew because he died when I was four. I would turn to my mother and ask her one more time if she was sure, if she was positive, he was really black, like black-black, not just drop-in-the-bucket black, because my grandpa Harry Dennis was even fairer than my mother. He looked like the KFC founder, Colonel Sanders.

My mother wore a lot of jewellery when I was younger—chunky silver rings and hoops and sterling silver bangles that made her jingle like a gypsy. I loved the way her bangles curled around her arm like silver branches, the way they sang as she moved, the way they felt cool against my skin when she held me. So I pulled her big and chunky silver jewellery, her art deco and hippie-style rings, from her drawer of accessories and wore them as often as she let me. When she eventually bought me silver bangles of my own, I was ecstatic.

Gold looks cheap, I would say of the massive, shiny, yellow hoops black musicians and actresses wore on television. My brother and sister told me that gold was more expensive.

"You wear silver because you have white friends," Damon explained.

Damon and Skye both wore gold. They had black friends and dressed like the black people we watched on variety shows and sitcoms—my brother in sporty baseball caps and tattered jeans with solid colour blocks; my sister in brightly coloured pants and shoes, with permed, straight hair and bangs like MC Lyte.

Look at Mom, they would say in defence of their claim. In addition to the musical, silver-branch bangles my mother wore, my mother's friends were white also. Which is why it was so hard for me to understand why my mother went to Howard University following her senior year of high school, given what was going on in the country.

In April 1970, President Nixon announced that American soldiers fighting in Vietnam would be sent into Cambodian territory. It was an action that contradicted what Americans wanted— an end to U.S. involvement in the overseas conflict. Protests erupted on campuses across the country, the most historic at Kent State University. It was a campus located forty-five minutes from Toledo, where my mother and father lived and were then dating.

On May 4, 1970, thousands of students gathered at the bottom of a hill near one of the Kent University buildings for a large protest. A patrolman read an order instructing the students to disperse or risk arrest. Protesters threw stones at the patrolman's car, and the National Guard (a branch of the American Armed Forces, designated for issues of state and national security) was summoned. Guardsmen guided students to an open area, before returning back up the hill, in the direction where they had started. When the National Guardsmen reached the top of the hill, they turned and fired their rifles. Some fired into the air; others fired directly into the crowd of unarmed students. Four white students were killed and nine others were wounded. Of those shot, the nearest were more than two hundred feet away from the shooters.

Eleven days later, at an all-black college in Jackson, Mississippi, a rumour spread across campus that a black mayor from a nearby city had been murdered. The National Guard, along with local enforcement, was called on to assist as angry students gathered together on the campus. When an unidentified popping sound was heard, they opened fire on the students. Two students were killed and twelve others were wounded during the massacre at Jackson State College. Many blamed the lack of attention and publicity given to this event, in comparison to the Kent State media frenzy, on the race of those killed and wounded at all-black Jackson State College.

The events at Kent State and Jackson College energized college students across the country. Leaders of the National Student Association—a student group focused on social change and vehemently opposed to the war in Vietnam—called for a "nationwide strike of indefinite duration." Members of the NSA marched on the nation's capital and protested in major cities. They staged candlelight vigils and barricaded highways. On the walls of campus buildings, students spray-painted black fists and wrote: "Shut it down" and "Free the Panthers". At the University of San Diego, twenty-three-year-old George Winne poured kerosene on his clothing and set himself on fire. As he burned to death, he held a sign that read: "In the name of God, end the war." Many feared a revolution.

Over 30,000 members of the National Guard were sent to more than a dozen states to help maintain order, as protests took place on nearly 80 per cent of American campuses. The unrest reflected the nation's worst ideological split since the Civil War. But President Nixon attributed the chants, marches, and rock throwing to the work of rebellious communists.

After her senior year of high school, amid this atmosphere of racial intolerance and conflict, my mother decided to attend Howard University—an all-black college in the heart of the nation's dissonant capital.

Howard University was founded in 1867, soon after the end of the Civil War. At the time my mother enrolled, it was described as "the largest of the centers for higher education for Negroes."

As I spoke to my mother about the choice she made to attend Howard University in 1970, I thought of the political fervour during the civil rights movement and Vietnam activism. Part of me was proud of the decision, jealous even. It implied a sense of black awareness and political savvy that maybe I was missing when I went away to college. Howard University and the University of Guelph couldn't have been more different.

I wanted to go to the University of Guelph because I was going to study liberal arts. That's what I was good at—English, drama, history, the social sciences. Only the University of Guelph was predominately white.

When I told my father I was going there, he seemed surprised. "Isn't that for farmers?" he asked.

"It was once an agricultural college," I said. "Now they offer everything."

Skye and Damon came to visit and commented on how *country* it felt, how different it was from the urban campuses they had chosen, how the environment was so *well suited* to me but would never do for them. What Damon and Skye were really saying was that there were a lot of white people—that in that atmosphere, I would feel totally comfortable. And I did. Which at the time confused me even more.

Before he died, my fair-skinned grandfather is known to have said that if he were to come back to earth again he would ask to be so dark that there would be no question about it. I wondered if that was part of the reason my mother went to Howard. Was she looking to remove questions of blackness? At seventeen, was my mother as confused as I had been?

My mother's time at Howard was brief. It was something she rarely talked about, which is not like her. She's usually open, forthright. If Portsmouth was where my father had hidden his memories of regret, then Howard University in Washington D.C. was where my mother was hiding her most revealing stories.

In the heart of the nation's capital, during a visit there in 2004, I would uncover the truth about what happened in 1970. In the secrets my father and mother never wanted to reveal, I would begin to resolve my questions about history and blackness.

17

THE DISTRICT OF COLUMBIA is considered neutral territory—the land it occupies acquired from two neighbouring states, Virginia and Maryland, to create a political epicentre that reflects the ideal context for democracy. I was sitting in the backseat of my aunt Derryl Stewart's purple PT Cruiser when I saw it for the first time in a hot 2004 summer.

Outside of Dee Dee's Maryland neighbourhood there was a green road sign with a white line down the middle. It was posted on the curb of a T-shaped intersection, where we stopped momentarily, during our first tour of the city. It read—with corresponding arrows—D.C. left, VA right. I looked to the right and thought with some measure of discomfort, so *that's* Virginia.

When I was younger, I would stow away for hours in my room and consume children's fiction in one sitting. I read books like *Shoelaces and Brussels Sprouts*, books that came from our local Christian bookstore and had clear, moral messages. Eventually I moved on to historic romance novels, which had titles like *Confederate Bride* and *Captive Belle Amongst the Rebels*. They were about elegant belles in corsets and gowns awaiting handsome Confederate suitors. They told of carriage rides and columned plantation houses with winding staircases, cordial parlours, balls, and extravagant visits to big cities. The stories were set in lush, green Georgia and the sunny Carolinas, but the ones I remember most took place in the historic state of Virginia—in cities like Alexandria, Arlington, and Richmond.

The settings and the atmosphere were not places that black people like me enjoyed historically, although initially I missed that. And when I began to read other kinds of novels, and researched history, I came to resent those old Civil War novels—the yes, ma'ams and no, mastahs, the wild slave, the subservient servant.

Decades after reading those novels, that reminded me of why I was visiting Washington, D.C. I needed to correct the things I had seen or read that had shaped an inaccurate view of myself and of history. I stared out the window as Dee Dee drove through D.C. She pointed out the White House, the African American Museum, the Museum of the American Indian. But there was one place in particular that I wanted to visit.

The National Mall in Washington is nothing like what we call malls in Canada. It's located outdoors, across acres of landscape; there are monuments to every war America has fought in, statues and flags marking contracts of diplomacy and international alliances; there are words of wisdom from America's most prominent leaders etched in the walls and stone pathways.

The day of our visit, the park was quiet, the sun beige and hazed behind murky clouds. Brief bouts of wind slipped through the trees as we made our way through the labyrinth of paths. I had seen the Lincoln Memorial Reflecting Pool on TV and in movies, but in person it was not clear or pool-like. It was cloudy and brown with geese gliding along the surface—their webbed feet paddling through the thick pond water. As I walked towards the Lincoln Memorial and climbed the massive stairway, I soaked in the history.

The Lincoln Memorial holds a statue of Abraham Lincoln in the shadow of a building that looks like the Parthenon. It's chalky and white, colourless, as though it were carved out of bone or painted in chalk dust. Inside the building, a gigantic Lincoln sits on a large, wide chair that faces the National Mall with an expression that's meant to appear thoughtful, but seems stoic, distant. Over his head an inscription reads: "In this temple, as in the hearts of men, the memory of Abraham Lincoln is enshrined forever."

Dee Dee and my mother made their way around the monument, reading the speeches and inscriptions. I stood there and thought about that inscription, about the forever of memory. I thought about the things that I wanted to reconstruct from the bones of my history. I thought about what I wanted my children to remember someday about what our family had encountered in this country. I looked at the stone steps we had climbed, the water that stretched out before the Lincoln Memorial. I thought of Dr. Martin Luther King Jr. standing below on one of the landings. I thought of the incredible urgency he must have felt, as a result of all that had not yet occurred in the years since Lincoln signed his proclamation.

> *One hundred years later, the Negro still is not free. One hundred years later, the life of the Negro is still sadly crippled by the manacles of segregation and the chains of discrimination. One hundred years later, the Negro lives on a lonely island of poverty in the midst of a vast ocean of material prosperity.*

The I Have a Dream speech had always sung of hope when I was younger—little boys and girls who would one day go to school together; freedom that would one day stretch from north to south, savannahs to mountaintops. Now I heard the great heartache, the crippling manacles, the heavy chains in King's discourse.

My father had lived on a lonely island of poverty, like Dr. King and so many others, and the silent waves that had passed between us as a result of those hardships—hardships that I never understood or acknowledged, because he spared me from them.

John Carlos—the Olympian who was banned from Olympic competition in 1968 because of his demonstration on the podium—spoke at an event in Toronto a few months after I sat down with my father. He shared stories about the difficulties he faced leading up to, and following, the Mexico City Olympics. He spoke about the conditions in America, and the disagreements black athletes had about the best method of protest. He spoke about a meeting he attended in regard to the potential boycott, a meeting where he met Dr. Martin Luther King Jr.

At the meeting, Dr. King told John Carlos that a boycott of the Olympics by black American athletes would be like a stone thrown in water. The initial event would cause a splash, followed by large and small ripples that would expand and stretch to the shoreline. It would impact people, influence thinking, change history.

The podium protest in Mexico City wasn't the massive and unified boycott that Carlos and Dr. King had hoped for. But Carlos's and Smith's actions after King's death still made an impact. It forced people to acknowledge what was happening in America; it forced people to consider why John Carlos and Tommie Smith were willing to sacrifice everything to draw attention to their struggles.

Perhaps the good choices men like my father made in small, segregated neighbourhoods were all like that—stones of various sizes thrown in water. Actions performed out of a dire need to improve the way things were—to affect the generation after them.

As I stood in the same spot where Dr. King had thrown stones at a nation that refused to embrace him, I realized I was the product of stone-throwing ripples forty years later. My life was the dream, the hope imagined by generations who suffered. I needed to pick up my own stones and throw them in the water.

18

THE MONTHS my mother spent at Howard University, starting in September 1970, is a time my parents never talk about. When I've asked my parents about that time, they both say: Let's not talk about that. So when Dee Dee suggested we visit the Howard University campus on our second day in Washington I agreed immediately.

"Are you coming with us?" I asked my mother.

"I only went there for a year," she said. She continued to stare out the passenger-side window.

I wanted to tell her that her short tenure at the school was the very reason I wanted to go, that regrets weren't so bad if you could figure out what you were supposed to learn, how to make them purposeful. Instead, I sat back in the car and listened to the rubber tires roll across the pavement.

My mother pointed her finger towards a cluster of buildings on the other side of a fenced-in lake-like body of water and said dryly, "There's Howard." She had been oddly quiet since Dee Dee set out for Howard.

"You had a lake on campus?" I said.

"It's a reservoir," Dee Dee said.

My mother huffed. "That would explain the rats."

That was the one thing my mother had shared with me about her time at Howard—there were rats in her dormitory. My mother detested rodents. When my father teased her with stories about the fat rats he'd seen in the projects, my mother would cringe and shake her head until he stopped talking or until he was laughing too hard to continue.

Dee Dee parked the car on a side street and we followed her on foot towards the main buildings on the Howard University campus. We passed a young black girl pushing a child in a stroller, tight jeans and a small shirt squeezing the folds of her belly, bright pink bra straps hanging out; the child held a red soda cup. His face was round, his expression grim and cranky as the girl spoke loudly on her cellphone. Y'all ain't heard nuthin', girl, I tell you, y'all don't even know what I's about to do 'bout it, as she kissed her teeth intermittently. Two girls walked by with hair extensions coloured red and copper, large, gold jewellery ringing from their ears and wrists as they discussed the latest celebrity gossip.

Near the campus there were old convenience stores and pizza-shop/liquor-store combos operating out of two-storey houses. There were fenced-in vacant lots with weedy yards and brick walls and street signage marred by graffiti.

The university buildings on the other side of the street, however, were beautiful—grand architecture surrounded by perfect lawns and meticulous gardens. As we stood in front of one of America's oldest and most prominent black universities, I tried to consolidate the images—the beauty of the campus and the roughness of the surrounding neighbourhood. I tried to imagine my mother at seventeen, standing on that street in 1970, her cream-coloured face surrounded by strangers. I closed my eyes and I tried, but I just couldn't see it.

While my mother was away at Howard University, my father had begun his second season as the starting quarterback for the

University of Toledo Rockets. In the first game of the season, the Rockets beat East Carolina University 35–2. They went on to win the next five games, defeating archrival Bowling Green University 20–0 in front of more than 21,000 Rocket fans at the Glass Bowl. After a game in Dayton, Ohio—a game my grandmother attended—the following article appeared in Toledo's local paper.

The Blade
November 15, 1970

SNOW, MUD, DAYTON CAN'T STOP ROCKETS
Jim Taylor

Great armies have been slowed to a crawl by mud and snow, but the University of Toledo's goo-splattered legions marched on Saturday.

Wading through glop, slop, and gloom, TU boomed past University of Dayton 31–7, as 7,163 spectators shivered in a game-long snowfall at Baujan Field.

The only way anyone could recognize the Rockets at the finish was by their consistently skilful performance.

Otherwise, they looked like figurines, dripped with a thick, brown coating which covered their once-white shirts and midnight blue pants.

It was the 21st straight triumph for Toledo over two seasons, and the 10th this year with one contest remaining . . .

Curiously, the Rockets had no fumbles and no interceptions with sure-handed Chuck Ealey at the controls.

The Rockets finished the 1970 regular season with a hometown victory against Colorado State, completing their second consecutive unbeaten season—no losses or ties in their perfect record. One writer described the team and their ability to face fierce opponents, their calm in the midst of overwhelming elements, as having an *aura of invincibility*. But when my father returned to Toledo after the holidays with his second MVP trophy from another Tangerine Bowl victory in Florida, Coach Lauterbur announced that he was leaving the Rockets to coach the University of Iowa. Fans and players alike wondered how it would affect the team and their winning record.

As the ice and snow of winter melted into the spring of 1971, there were other changes that were about to take place while my mother was living at Howard University in the Harriet Tubman Quadrangle.

The Quad is a residence complex made up of five red brick buildings on D.C.'s Howard University campus. Pathways intertwine throughout the complex and a small brick wall lines the front lawn. In the early seventies, it included an all-girls residence called Crandall Hall.

As we walked past the wall during our summer visit in 2004, my mother ran her fingertips across the concrete that topped the brick wall. For the first time since arriving on campus she smiled.

"I spent a lot of time on this wall. We used to sit here between classes," she said.

My mother grazed her fingers along the bricks, feeling the gritty texture.

My mother lived in the only room on the first floor of Crandall Hall throughout her first year of college. Her roommate hurt her ankle during the first week of classes and had gone home soon after. For a number of weeks, my mother was all by herself. Her second roommate, Cathy Smith, lived nearby and didn't register for residence until six weeks into the semester.

Cathy was fair like my mother, an effervescent arts major. They got along well and spent time together, but it didn't ease the uncertainty my mother had already started to feel about her decision to attend Howard University. She wondered if coming to Howard had been wise, if she could do three more years at the all-black college in the busy capital. For reasons she did not fully understand at the time, she didn't feel happy. One night in April, my mother remembers receiving an unexpected phone call.

"Hello? . . . No, this is Cathy . . . Yeah, one second." She holds the phone out to her roommate. "It's for you."

"Hello?"

"Hey."

"Chuck?"

"Yeah." ·

My mother sits down on her bed and faces the wall, head down as she presses the receiver against her lips and lowers her voice casually. "How are you?"

"Mmm. Okay."

Awkward silence.

"Football's going well?" she says. "I mean I know it's only spring. But . . . it's going well?"

"Yup. Yeah."

"Good."

Cathy looks at her roommate and waves her hand, encouraging her to hurry.

My mother looks away and says gently, "Chuck?"

"Yeah?"

"Is everything okay?"

"I just wanted to call to—to tell you about Bryant."

She sits up, voice back at full volume. "What do you mean? What about Bryant?"

They had hardly spoken since the holidays and she suddenly wished they had spoken more often, that they weren't on the phone so this wasn't so awkward. She wished she could see him, see what he was trying to say but couldn't.

"Chuck?!"

"Bryant passed away."

Another awkward silence.

"I . . . I don't know what to say."

"He made it longer than we expected."

She chews her lip. He was always so matter-of-fact, even-keeled, even now. But he's not okay. He can't be. She wants to say something to make him feel better. *Something. Anything.*

"How's your mom?"

He pauses, clears his throat. "She's holding up."

"I'm so sorry."

"I just wanted to let you know."

She nods, forgetting he can't see her.

"And the funeral. Don't worry," he says. "I know you have school."

She wonders if he's being considerate or if he's saying this because he'd rather she not be there. "But . . ."

"It's okay," he says. "I understand."

You understand what? She tries to say something meaningful, helpful, but she can sense that he's anxious.

"I got to go," he says quickly.

"Of course. Yeah. You must be . . . busy."

"Ya. It's busy."

"Chuck?"

"Yeah?"

"I'm really sorry."

She places the phone down gently and thinks of the little boy she met in Dayton a few months earlier. He was so full of energy, full of joy. It had her believing maybe it wasn't so bad, maybe he wasn't actually dying.

She lies down on her bed, phone clutched to her chest, and cries—shoulders shaking, face pressed into her pillow.

———————

I lived in a building at the University of Guelph that had been converted from a women's hospital to an all-girls' residence when the university opened. Ivy hung down the brick exterior and crept around the windows like lace foliage. The interior was renovated with new carpet and new furniture. It looked like the university dormitories I had seen in movies. I still miss it. I occasionally return to visit.

At Macdonald Hall, young women pored over papers and textbooks, and ran doorway to doorway in the face of real and imagined emergencies. They sprawled out on beds and sat cross-legged in the hallways in sweatpants and pajamas. Most of the girls were from small towns in Ontario that I had never heard of—Arthur, Tilsonburg, St. Clements. I was the only black girl in my residence, as far as I can remember.

One of the girls admitted to me one day, when we were a few weeks into the semester, that she didn't know very many black people. I was her only black friend. The few black people she knew from her small hometown were Trinidadian summer field hands or recent immigrants from Africa or the Caribbean—families that didn't stay long. Many of the other girls acknowledged similar experiences. They began to ask me questions—some interesting, some filled with a sheltered ignorance I recognized from my own knowledge limits.

One girl asked me why black girls were so mean to white girls, why they seemed unfriendly, angry. Another asked why the black boys in her town got into so much trouble. Another asked how I did my hair, why some black girls were able to grow theirs so quickly and change it day by day so dramatically. I fielded their questions as best I could. I shared what I was learning in my classes. I told them about the legacy of slavery, the African diaspora. I explained how the history of slavery affected the ways we saw one another. Sometimes what white people saw as anger was hurt and frustration over things they didn't, and maybe couldn't, understand. I told them what little I knew about hair weaves and hair extensions. It was the first time I had ever been the expert on blackness.

I was someone they could relate to because we were living together, because we had all lived in white worlds that had their similarities. I was also part of a world they had never known and would never be able to inhabit—one that they were curious about, but had never been able to navigate.

When my mother came home in 1971, just after Bryant's death, she wasn't sure whether she would go back to Howard or not. What she was certain about was that she wanted things to be different between her and my father. When she got back she was prepared to tell him everything, to catch up and do things better now that she was back in town. She waited at her house on Searles Road, giddy with excitement. It had been months since they'd seen one another—a long time since they had had a good conversation.

She smoothed her skirt and straightened her blouse, hands damp and shaky. When my father appeared at the door, she opened it wide and slid her arms around his waist. She let her ear rest against his chest as they stood there for a moment. He seemed taller, broader. When she finally let go, he moved towards one of the couches and she followed. It had been a hard year and she could see that on his face. He had changed. Or maybe she was different.

My father taps his long fingers together as my mother sits down next to him.

"I don't think this is working," he says.

She tries to stay poised, tries to hide her disappointment, as her stomach drops inside of her. He's looking down at the carpet and she needs to stay calm and collected.

"Oh?"

"I think it's best if we just, you know, do our own thing," he says.

She smiles a sad grin that pushes up her tears, because all she hears is what she learned about irony from her English classes.

"Ya. Ya, you're probably right," she says.

He looks at her, her head now lowered, and thinks about the difference one year has made, back to the first time he saw her in front of this same house, back when he told John Saunders she was the woman he was going to marry. He remembers the way it felt to share Bryant's life with someone. It's just not working.

"Where will you be this summer?" she asks.

"Columbus."

She nods. "That's cool."

"Yeah."

"I'm working at a summer camp," she says, even though he didn't ask.

"I'm sure I'll see you around," he says.

"Oh sure. Yeah. Of course. I'm sure we'll see each other at some point."

When he finally stands up to leave and they say their goodbyes, my mother watches him walk away and drive off before closing the door again. She sits on the couch and holds a pillow to her face to muffle the sound of her heartbreak.

"Did you think that when you left for school that everything was going to be okay?" I asked my mother.

"Yeah. I think so. I was young. I didn't have a clue," she said, eyes fixed on the bottom of her empty mug of coffee.

"When I went away to school, there were all these other people and I was far away from home. So . . . " Her voice trailed off.

"All these *other people*?" I said.

"Other guys," she said, her words thrown out like a broken, glass heirloom—cracked with regret, shattered with that impossible wish to go back and make it unhappen.

"That you . . . dated?"

"Mmmhmm."

"While you were dating Dad?"

One short, slow nod. "Mmmhmm."

"And was he . . . dating other girls?"

"Yes, but I didn't know that."

"And he didn't know that you were dating other guys either."

"Right."

I stopped for a moment as I tried to collect my thoughts. My parents preached faithfulness and fidelity. They frowned on promiscuity. Watching their lives, the way they raised me, I had never imagined anything different. Only it wasn't their unfaithfulness that bothered me. They were young after all. I was disappointed by all of the things I didn't know about them—all of the things that changed everything.

"We kept missing each other that summer," my father told me. "When I came back home for the weekend to Toledo, she was at camp. When she came back from camp, I was in Columbus."

A few weeks before my mother was expected to head back to college, she finally got a hold of my father. My father couldn't remember the conversation he had with my mother at her house when she got back from Howard, but he did remember the conversation they had just before his senior year started.

"She called me and said, 'Before I go back to university, when you come back from Columbus, I'd like to talk to you.' And I kind of said, you know what, there's no use talking to me if you're going back."

I laughed and shook my head when my father said this. It was the familiar blunt self-assuredness that characterized all of his conversation style. My father was a verbal sniper—focused and direct with a ready-aim-fire delivery.

"When I met with her, she asked if there was a chance that we could get back together," he told me. "I was immediately defensive because I knew she was going back to university and I said, 'You know what, there's just no way that between me being here and all that's going on around me, and you being there, that this will work if you go back to Howard. It just won't work.' And she said no, that if there was a chance that we could be together and stay together she was willing to not return to Howard."

My father leaned back against the couch, hands clasped behind his head, his eyes wide as he remembered all over again.

"That kind of floored me because, I mean, she had a scholarship. It caught me off guard. I told her again, if you go back, we don't have a chance. If you're here, there's a good chance we will be together and have something going. Then I said the rest is up to you and your mom, your family. I don't want you to give up your scholarship to stay here and think that we're going to be together, because that may not happen."

When I left for my last year of university, three months after Mark and I met, I warned him that school would be the most important priority in my life for the next eight months. I told him that I wouldn't be home every weekend, and that I would let him know when he could visit. It was my last year with my friends. It was my last chance to get the grades I needed for grad school.

When my father shared about how he and my mother got back together, I heard in his account not the similarities with my mother I was accustomed to, but the confident and resolute will of my father. Was that the reason we clashed for so long, riddled by stubborn silences? Was I a conversational sniper also?

I was starting to think about what my father and I had in common, instead of what divided us, when my father turned to me and asked me for something. He admitted there was something he had never known, something he had always been curious about, but never had the courage to ask that he wanted me to ask my mother about.

"What made you call him that summer?" I said to my mother, when we were sitting in her kitchen a few days later.

My mother shrugged and picked a crumb off the table with just her index finger. She wiped it against her napkin.

"I think after I thought about the year and assessed the fact that I had probably made some really poor choices during the time I had been at school, I realized that I needed to put more effort into the relationship with your father to see if anything could actually develop."

"So you didn't go back to Howard?"

She nodded.

"How did Grandma take it?"

My grandma Dorothy Dennis had a university degree from an all-black college in Louisiana; she completed a master's degree in social work at the University of Chicago amidst civil rights activism. She was career-driven, self-motivated, and independent. She was also sceptical, critical, and stubborn.

"She cried," my mother said, as she crumpled the napkin in her hand. "She was worried I wouldn't finish school."

My grandmother had often told me about the scholarship my mother had but didn't use; but she never mentioned the tears she shed when her daughter left Howard University for a college football player. But in August of 1971, my mother did just that. She transferred to the University of Toledo and became the sophomore girlfriend of the university's star quarterback. It was a year that would turn out far differently than the one they buried behind them. It would also be the final year of college for both of them.

19

CHRISTINE BRENNAN was ten years old when my father became the starting quarterback for the University of Toledo Rockets. She watched my father lead the team to a series of victories that culminated in one undefeated season, then another. She witnessed an unbelievable winning streak that Rockets fans were desperate to keep going at the start of my father's senior year at college.

Christine's father, Jim Brennan, took her to Toledo Mudhen baseball games and Big Ten basketball games; he also took her to every Rockets home game my father played in from '69 to '71. Christine read every article in the local paper about the unbeaten Rockets. She would go on to study journalism, eventually becoming a sportswriter and broadcaster, largely because of the games she attended with her father.

In 1996, Brennan published a memoir entitled *The Best Seat in the House: A Father, a Daughter, a Journey Through Sports*. My father brought a copy home after a visit to Toledo, where he'd run into Christine at a local celebrity charity event. I read the first chapter, then the second, which focused on the Toledo football games when my father was the starting quarterback. I read the second chapter again and again. I studied it like a treasure map, retracing her experiences.

Toledo won the Tangerine Bowl again to finish the 1970
season undefeated and run its unbeaten streak to twenty-
three games. The Rockets were ranked twelfth in the nation
by the Associated Press, seventeenth by United Press Inter-
national. I was thrilled when I opened the paper and saw
the final polls. Nothing like this had ever happened to our
city, to our team . . . As the 1971 season opened, people
around the country were starting to notice.[3]

Before reading Brennan's words, I could only loosely imagine
those days from the newspaper articles and fuzzy, black-and-
white TV news footage. In Christine's memoir, I saw my father
through the eyes of a young girl who witnessed the excitement.
I saw my father and his senior teammates doing something that
invigorated football fans.

The whole town was watching each game, counting each victory. They were drawn to the nation's most popular sport with
passion and keen interest. They were hopeful, expectant. They
were mystified by the capabilities of the black quarterback they'd
dubbed the Wizard of Oohs and Aahs, because of what he could
do on the football field.

On October 11, 1971, thousands of fans huddled in their seats
at the Glass Bowl to watch my father face Ohio University as
seniors. Christine Brennan was in the stands, as was Joe Jares—a
sportswriter from the nation's most esteemed sports magazine,
Sports Illustrated. At halftime, the Rockets were up 17–14.

"That one was classic," Don Fair said, when we talked about
that final season. "We were lined up and we had called a play.
We were at the twenty-five-yard line. It was a night game and
your dad was in his cadence. I was in my stance. He just looked
over at me and winked. He just kind of looked at me and I
knew what he wanted. I ran a quick slant and he delivered the

ball. I dodged a couple of guys and scored."

Don Fair also made a name for himself during his time with the Rockets. He became known as Sticky Fingers. Rumour has it he never dropped a pass in all three years as a Rockets wide receiver.

Don Fair's catch was not enough to secure victory during that last OU matchup. With four minutes left to play in the game, the score was just 31–28 for the Rockets. Ohio University was thirty-seven yards from the end zone and it was fourth and three. Ohio University was one field goal away from ending the Rockets' streak of victories with a tie game.

Twelve-year-old Brennan and *Sports Illustrated*'s Joe Jares both watched expectantly—ready to witness a tie that would break the winning streak. Ohio set up for the last play of the series— a thirty-seven-yard field goal. On the snap from centre to set up the kick, Ohio University fumbled the ball and the Rockets defence recovered it. When the clock ran out, the University of Toledo Rockets had secured another incredible victory.

Sports Illustrated
October 11, 1971

HOLY TOLEDO! CHUCK EALEY NEARLY LOST ONE
Joe Jares

The candlepower in the Glass Bowl is so low that at night the place is more suitable for séances or Halloween parties than the home games of the University of Toledo Rockets. But they have this hobgoblin quarterback named Chuck Ealey who flits in and out of the shadows to elude tacklers then zings the ball right on the button to one of

his receivers, all of whom can see in the dark like owls.
His teammates have an almost mystical belief in his ability
to get them out of any jam. "The remarkable thing about
Ealey is that he has positive thought waves." And well he
might. In 57 games of varsity football in high school and
college, Charles Ealey Jr. has never lost.

After the game, Joe Jares asked my father if he thought any
opponent would ever be able to beat him.

"Well . . . some negative thoughts do protect you from
becoming overconfident." Then he smiled, and the positive thought waves shot out of him like gamma rays. You
knew that inside his head he really couldn't picture such
a thing.

"I never saw the game in the perspective of a countdown," my
father told me, when I asked him about the close game against
OU and the interview with Jares. "I never even knew a count until
someone put it in a newspaper. One day you'd finish the game
and the next day you'd have films. 'This is where you messed
up, here's what you did well,' the coaches would say. 'Here's the
team you're playing next week.' You never had time to appreciate where you were. It never really crossed my mind. There was
no ESPN. The only television network that covered college football was ABC. They always covered Michigan State, Ohio State,
Notre Dame. No other schools were on television. We were kind
of an unknown entity."

Close games and last-minute victories were not the only way
my father and the unknown Rockets would become part of history. The Toledo Rockets would appear on major news channels
when their streak intersected with one of America's greatest
sports tragedies.

On November 14, 1970, most of the players on Marshall University's football team, along with their wives, the coaching staff, and several team supporters boarded a plane at Tri-State Airport in North Carolina en route to their hometown of Huntington, West Virginia—a town of 80,000 people, six hours south of Toledo, a town my father had visited as a teenager because of a dance show that was filmed there. On that foggy, wet day in November, that plane crashed into a hill, two miles off the runway. All seventy-five passengers, including thirty-seven players and their coaches, died in the crash.

Christine Brennan remembered it vividly.

> *It was the worst disaster in U.S. sports history. We heard about it on the news on the radio and read the story on the front page of* The Blade *the day after it happened. Those players from Marshall had played in the Glass Bowl in late September; their bench was just a few feet in front of us. Now they were all dead. It was hard for me, for any of us, to fathom.*[4]

Amid controversy over whether or not the college should revive the football program, a man by the name of Jack Lengyel accepted the daunting task of rebuilding the team in time for the next season. He believed that the return to college football was important to the town's recovery. With less than two months to prepare for spring practice, and with a full roster and four new coaches to hire, Lengyel managed the seemingly impossible. A squad of mostly freshmen and sophomores and a brand new coaching staff came together in the spring, ready in time for the 1971 season. My father and his teammates faced the new Marshall University roster on the one-year anniversary of the tragic plane crash.

The inexperienced Marshall team was expected to flounder against the repeat conference champions, but my father was plagued with a sore arm—an injury he had suffered one week earlier. Coach John Murphy, the new head coach for the Rockets, was uncertain about what to do with his star quarterback. My father was capable of playing, but given the youthful Marshall roster, Murphy wondered if he should rest him.

Following the tribute service held before the game to honour the lives that were lost and those who were touched by the tragedy, Coach Murphy decided that despite my father's injury, he would begin the game by starting my father. Coach Murphy wanted to respect and honour the fans and the Marshall team, past and present, by beginning the game with their best roster.

While the Rockets would go on to win 43–0, and my father would only play in the first quarter, Murphy's decision to start my father became incredibly significant. At the end of the regular season that senior year, my father had started in every one of his thirty-four games as the University of Toledo's quarterback. He had never lost a matchup.

"Were there any games where you thought you were going to lose?" I asked my father.

My father looked out the window. My mother's wind chimes were singing and dancing outside in the chilly winds of winter.

"There were two games in my senior year that were probably pivotal moments in keeping the streak alive—one against Villanova when it was 7–7. I took and threw the pass to my roommate Glyn Smith and he caught it and we got a field goal and won it, 10–7. Although before the field goal, I still didn't think we were going to lose."

"How much time was left?"

"Thirty-five seconds."

I shook my head in disbelief.

"There was never a time where I thought we were going to lose," he said.

It was the same confidence he conveyed when he told the story about how events led him to Toledo—an internal belief in the face of something that seemed unlikely, unattainable, or impossible; it was the same confidence and determination that led him to pick up those stones and launch them at the train that ran along tracks that divided two neighbourhoods. He kept throwing those stones, because he knew that hitting the "N" was always possible.

"There was a homecoming game against Western Michigan," my father added. "We were down 24–7 at halftime. People were kind of—" He shook his head to illustrate pessimism. "But even then, I thought, no big deal, so what if we lose?" He focused his eyes on me and nodded. "That's what the problem was. The problem was that I was never pressured by what was considered a 'streak.' If we lost, we lost. There was always another game. I think it became more of a public perception of the streak. I don't even know if players on the team got caught up in counting the numbers. Nobody that I know of on the team was talking about it."

It didn't surprise me that my father wasn't thinking about it, given his ability to focus, aim with purpose—to overcome what was typical, likely, and probable. It was hard to believe that no one else was counting, that no one was tracking the games in scratched lines on locker doors and gym walls. I would have been counting, celebrating each milestone. I would have worried about what would happen if I let everyone down by losing.

"We knew we won. We didn't have to be told. We knew where we were. When you're on the field you don't have that same kind of viewpoint that people in the stands have, like Christine, watching it happening."

I was caught up in the most magical of relationships between a fan and a team that 1971 season. At thirteen, I threw everything I had, my heart and soul, into the Rockets, and

*they were repaying me—repaying Dad, Kate, Jim, all of us—
in ways I never could have imagined. The louder I cheered,
the more the team won. The Rockets never, ever disappointed
me. They never let me down. They always rewarded my
devotion with more victories, with more happiness. How
often can a fan say that about a sports team?*[5]

My father took the field on December 28, 1971, for the final game
of his college career at the Tangerine Bowl in Orlando, Florida.
Over 16,000 fans filled the stands—including thirteen-year-old
Christine Brennan who had received two tickets to the game and
a trip to Florida with her father for Christmas. She would witness the final appearance of those senior athletes—men who had
delivered thirty-four wins in thirty-four games in three years of
Rockets football.

At the end of the first quarter, after a Richmond field goal
split the uprights, the Spiders were ahead by three. In the second
quarter, Richmond had the ball again and was pressed against
their end zone when their quarterback was tackled. The ball
tumbled on the field and Rockets defenceman Mel Long recovered it for a touchdown. When my father drove his team to the
Richmond end zone with passes to Glyn Smith and Don Fair,
the Rockets secured a score of 14–3 at halftime. They sealed
their victory later in the game with two additional touchdowns
for a final score of 28–3. They were 35 and 0.

The Blade
January 1, 2001

Their banner read "No. 1 In the World," the pragmatic
evaluation of a group of loyalists as they paraded through
the stadium seats in Orlando, Florida on December 28,
1971. The University of Toledo football team had just

defeated Richmond, 28–3, in the Tangerine Bowl. But this was more than the establishment of a beachhead, more than a single battle in the shaping of a war. This was to be a conquest of the most dramatic period in a rich TU athletic history.

There were 19 seniors on that 1971 TU football team who never lost a collegiate game and can still lay claim to being part of the greatest era in Mid-American Conference football history.[6]

"I didn't want to leave the field," Don Fair said. "I remember coming into the locker room and it was the most awful feeling. It was the best feeling but the most awful feeling. I didn't want to take my uniform off. I didn't even want to take my wristbands off. I didn't want to take the eye-black off. I was just like, you know what, this cannot be over—this group of people, this thing that we just did, this cannot be over. We were twenty-one years old and I was taking it off, going, this is never going to happen again, you know. I'm not going to be putting these pads on again; we're not going to be together as a team again. It just can't end like this."

We sat side by side in the section with the Toledo fans who had made the trip to Orlando. I wore a blue and yellow Toledo button. The Rockets won easily, 28–3. I never stopped cheering. But as the clock wound down, I strangely started to wish time would go the other way. Could we turn the hourglass over and let it start again? I wanted to add time to the clock to watch this team, not subtract it.

When the game ended, I could feel tears welling in my eyes. I looked at Dad. He put his arm around me.

"That's the end of an era, honey," he said.

"Dad, we'll never see them play again."

He nodded. "But you'll have a whole new team to cheer for next year."

The thought of next year, without these players, sent tears streaming down my cheeks. As the crowd began to file out around us, we remained in our seats, Dad's arm pulling me tighter toward him, his other arm reaching for a handkerchief in his pocket. All those great times we had had with our incredible, unbeatable team had come to an end.

"There will always be another kickoff," Dad said, trying to reassure me, but it seemed far away that late-December evening in Orlando. I was caught up in the memory of those three years of football. Thirty-five games I had watched, or listened to, or worried over. Three consecutive years of football games. The Rockets had won them all.[7]

I wept as I read Brennan's account of that last game in Orlando—the hard, uncontrollable tears that led to sobs and broken breaths. Although initially I didn't know why I reacted so ardently. When I sat down to write a letter to Christine, to thank her for her heart-wrenching account, I continued to cry as my fingers pressed against the keyboard. I suddenly knew why I was so emotional.

Christine knew my father in a way I never would—the sound of his feet tiptoeing on the grass, the spin of his passes when they hung in the air like kites. She knew the look in his eyes when the score was close and time was winding down—that flash thrill, absent of doubt; that inconceivable confidence. She knew the excitement of a place I longed to be—right there on the sidelines, cheering victory after victory.

I wish I could have been there to watch those games at the Glass Bowl, in those stands in Orlando. I wish I had seen my father play football. I wish I could know that part of him.

I visited an old church with my family in Toledo's black neighbourhood a few years after reading Christine Brennan's memoir. It was a church on a cobblestone road with weathered pews and high ceilings.

After the service, the reverend approached my father. He told my father that he was the reason he had come to Toledo. In the early seventies, he was faced with a choice about where he might settle. When his brother told him that UT had a black quarterback, he decided to come to Toledo. He had watched my father play football at the Glass Bowl, inspired by each victory. As he looked at my father and shook his hand, placing it firmly between both of his rough palms, his face reflected the joy of those memories—his eyes shining as though watching my father as a young man forty years earlier.

A tiny, old woman joined us, nodding at the reverend's comments. She slipped her arm through mine, squeezing me gently. She smiled up at my father, star-struck.

"When each football season ended, I didn't know what to do with myself," she said. "Those Rockets are the reason I'm here."

Despite his undefeated record, my father still believes his time at Toledo was nothing unusual. No one seems to be able to explain or convey to him just how extraordinary it is. Amid the victories and his incredible feats, there were also difficult personal tragedies: there was unprecedented social unrest that was felt across the country. My father doesn't see that it's that combination of events and occurrences that makes his undefeated legacy at the University of Toledo so phenomenal.

20

I TURNED TWENTY-FIVE the same year Matt Leinart and the USC Trojans prepared to make football history in southern California. I spent Christmas morning—the day before my birthday—with Mark, my parents, and Dee Dee, who had flown up to Canada for the holidays. Skye was in Florida visiting her in-laws, Damon in Texas visiting his. There were no kids to spoil and Santa-pretending, no oversized pajamas to watch my nephews swim around in while we captured every movement on camera. It was the first time I had been away from all of them at Christmas. I was feigning holiday joy and Christmas spirit when Skye called early that morning.

"How's the weather?" I said.

"Nice. Shorts, but not swimsuits."

She was in the town of Zephyr Hills, an hour outside of Tampa.

"What did you get?" she said.

"We haven't opened anything."

"It's 9 o'clock," she said.

My parents and Dee Dee were milling around, eating breakfast, clutching coffees. Mark was lying on the couch watching a show on home renovations. Eventually we got around to unwrapping the meagre pile of Christmas presents.

When everything was open, Mark handed me one more gift. He gave me an envelope as everyone sat waiting, watching. I opened the letter:

There's another gift—an automatic fish feeder, it said..

"A fish feeder?" I asked.

Mark loves fish. They're the only pets we both agree on, although I rarely helped in the co-parenting of our cichlids.

"Keep reading," he said. His face was serious, but a grin was fighting against him.

We'll need the automatic fish feeder because we'll be in Florida for New Year's.

I read the words again and looked up at Mark.

"We're going to Florida?" I said and he nodded. "Does Skye know?"

He flipped a mocking hand in my direction. "No. You two can't keep secrets from each other," he said.

I ran into the kitchen and dialled back the most recent number. One ring.

"Hello?" Skye said.

"We're coming!"

"What?"

"Mark bought us tickets to Florida. We're coming down!"

"Seriously?" my sister said.

"We can watch the Rose Bowl together."

There was a pause, then a loud exhale. "Man, I hope he loses."

The year my husband surprised me with a trip to Florida was the same year Matt Leinart quarterbacked his college football team to an undefeated season in his final year at the University of Southern California. He had lost his first game as a starter at USC but had won every game since—undefeated in his three subsequent seasons. He had won the Heisman Trophy and a

National Championship, and he wanted to win it again. He had finished his regular season and had one game left—the Rose Bowl. With thirty-four consecutive wins behind him, the Rose Bowl was also Leinart's last chance to tie my father's thirty-five straight victories.

Leinart and his USC Trojans would match up against the heavily predicted underdogs, Vince Young and the University of Texas Longhorns on the fourth day of 2006.

Fans and onlookers tuned in to the game, the fanfare and festivities, for the chance to watch history write itself into their memory. I watched in absolute horror. I prayed a prayer that I said out loud and over and over when the country predicted Leinart's Rose Bowl victory. *Dear God, Make him lose.*

In the weeks leading up to the game, TV announcers and sports media praised USC's California-Ken quarterback incessantly. He's a star, something special, something you don't see every day, they said. One for the record books. They mentioned the stakes, the unlikelihood of a Texas upset, the record Leinart would set when he won. But they didn't mention the current record holder until a few days before the game when my father was interviewed as part of ESPN's Rose Bowl pre-game coverage. I was angry and anxious. It seemed as though history was trying to forget him already. I prayed even harder for a Texas Longhorns victory as I tuned in for the ESPN interviews.

A woman in a hot-pink suit with matching pink lipstick sat at a desk in front of a backdrop of a locker room.

"So how does college football's perfect quarterback feel about possibly sharing the record?" she said rhetorically. "Only one man can answer that—Chuck Ealey, who joins us now."

The image on the screen split—my father appeared on the right side via satellite from Toronto, wearing a black shirt and a stylish, blue-grey sports coat.

"Chuck, why has that record stood for as long as it has—more than three decades?"

Bold white text in a black section at the bottom of the screen read: *Ealey's 35-Game Win Streak.*

"Well I think it's hard to do what we did at that time," my father said. He alluded to some of the influencing factors—timing, providence, how hard it is to stay healthy for three years with the weekly game schedule—before she asked a question my father had begun to encounter more regularly.

"So what do you want to see happen Wednesday night at the Rose Bowl?"

Footer: *Rooting For or Against Leinart.*

My father laughed and the screen changed, my father occupying the entire shot. He repeated his standard answer.

"I'd like to see a good game," he said with a small, polite grin. "I think the best they can do is tie the record, but I did everything I possibly could do and I hold nothing back from anybody else who would like to accomplish that same type of goal."

No, Dad. We want him to lose. I need him to lose. My father didn't understand why that was so important.

"Leinart will still have one loss," she said. "But you never suffered a loss in college. Does that change what this might mean to him?"

Action clips of Leinart, throwing the football, dodging opposing defensive players, appeared on the screen and the footer churned through the previous titles in rotation as my father explained that Leinart wouldn't be concerned about the record, *Ealey's 35-Game Win Streak,* that the count didn't matter. *Rooting For or Against Leinart.* It's the teammates, the experiences, and awards that Leinart should remember.

Then my father added a small point of clarification in a tone both tactful and humble. "It would be a record he would have that would go along with me. But he would have one loss."

Yes, Dad! You tell them! I said out loud in the family room in Florida.

Footer: *Leinart Challenges Consecutive Win Record.*

Records were made to be broken, people said in the commentary that followed the interview. I just kept praying, over and over: *Please, not this one.*

The day of the Rose Bowl, television announcers started early in the morning with more recaps of Leinart's fantastic senior season—his televised victories, his previous championship. They pointed out all of the reasons why a Vince Young victory was unlikely. The University of Texas's black quarterback was a Houston native, beloved for his urban, southern twang, his authentic homegrown appeal, his quickness on the football field. Young was from humble circumstances, raised by his grandmother and mother, his father was a convicted felon. The faceoff between Young and Leinart was slated as one of the most anticipated matchups in college football history.

Outside the Rose Bowl stadium, before the game Texas Longhorns fans pinched their middle and ring fingers against their thumb, index fingers and pinkies raised in the colloquial symbol of their bull-skeleton mascot. Trojan fans pointed in the air to show what they believed would once again be their final NCAA ranking. *Number 1 in the World*, their posters read.

Skye, her husband, my nephews, her in-laws, and Mark all settled in alongside me in the family room in Zephyr Hills to watch the game. I had been sitting on the loveseat watching coverage since breakfast. As the referees tossed the coin in the air to mark the start of the game, my sister squeezed my leg tightly.

"I'm so nervous!" she said.

I nodded, then breathed deeply.

A few weeks earlier, in a game where it seemed certain he would lose, I watched Leinart deliver a last-minute victory in the dying seconds of the game. I thought about what announcers and fans were saying of this team, this quarterback: This was meant to be. They were saying that Leinart was a natural-born leader—that a team like this particular group of Trojans were a one-in-a-million combination.

I thought of my father's games, how each win was more amazing than the next, how against the wind and the odds—and the mud—each victory seemed magical. It was a poignant time in history, and my father and his team accomplished something extraordinary. Was this the end of that story? Either Leinart and my father shared something supernatural, or my father possessed a unique and mystic talent.

When the Rose Bowl was finally under way, it seemed like the reporters were right. What announcers said was quickly evident. Leinart and his deep-bench team, including his Heisman award–winning running back, had more talent than the Longhorns. Even though the score was 16–10 at half in favour of the Longhorns, the Trojans were finding their footing. USC often had turnaround victories. They came back from half and quickly took the lead in a way that made victory seem imminent. If it was close near the end, everyone was certain USC would win it. I agreed. I had seen them do it.

By the end of the third quarter, USC was in the lead with a score of 24–23. My sisters-in-law and my nephews went to bed disappointed, followed by my football-fanatic brother-in-law. Texas was struggling. Vince Young seemed to be the only one fighting against the Trojans. Mark went to bed when the score reached 31–23 in favour of Leinart and the Trojans.

"Leinart's going to win," Mark said. "Poor Vince Young."

"It's not over," I said.

"Leinart will still be 35 and 1," he said.

He shrugged when I didn't respond because he didn't understand why that made me so angry. I couldn't explain it. It felt like a sharp rock was lodged in my throat, every gulp filled with sharp pressure.

With six minutes left on the clock, Skye and I were alone in the large, dark room, the only light the white glow of the television. She was sleeping, leaning over the arm of the couch, eyes closed, her mouth slightly open. I moved in front of the TV, cross-legged and wide-eyed.

Vince Young and the Longhorns were down by twelve points, with four minutes left to go in the game. The score was 38–26 for USC. Texas needed two touchdowns to win, to break Leinart's 34-game winning streak.

I prayed for a miracle as I sat there, my hands clasped in front of me, and as I did I was overcome with an unfamiliar feeling. It was the same feeling my father felt in those games where the elements and the opponents threatened to spoil his victory—a strong sense of possibility that smothered probability. In spite of the odds and the expectations, in spite of what time was telling me, I felt something I believed entirely.

It's not over.

On the other side of the country, Vince Young must have felt it as well. He moved his team 52 yards towards the end zone in eight plays, taking the last 17 yards himself for the touchdown.

USC 38, Texas 33.

USC got the ball with only a few minutes remaining. All they had to do was maintain possession to secure Leinart's thirty-fifth straight victory. They tried to drain the clock; they tried to let time write them into history. They called running plays, utilized Reggie Bush—their go-to, award-winning running back. But the Longhorns defence contained them, forcing the Trojans to give the ball back to Texas.

Vince Young and the Longhorn offence took the field for the last drive of the game, deep in their own territory, with less than a minute left to play. They were behind by one touchdown. Young was tall and quick, but compared to Leinart's polished approach he was less predictable, more erratic. They had only forty seconds to march that ball into the end zone.

Young can do it. He can still do it.

I kneeled on the tiled floor, hands clenched under my chin, my teeth rattling like marbles. With ten seconds on the clock, Texas was down by five points, ten yards away from a touchdown. It was fourth and five. This was Young's last chance to beat the odds for victory.

"All the dreams, all the hopes for the national championship come down to this play," the announcer said as the centre snapped the ball back and Vince Young gripped the leather gently with the balls of his fingers.

The stands roared loudly and the announcer's voice rose along with them as the seconds ticked down inside me: *10, 9 . . .*

"Young from the shotgun!"

Young's feet danced against the grass as his eyes searched from behind his facemask—*8, 7 . . .*

"He looks!"

A defender's arm stretched towards him. I held my breath as I watched a desperate teammate trying to help his quarterback—*6, 5.* But the defender was escaping—*4, 3 . . .*

"Under pressure!"

Young stepped to the side to avoid the reach of the defender and curled the ball under his arm, stepping forward—*2 . . .*

"He'll tuck it in to run!"

I leaned forward—*1 . . .*

"Young to the five!"

Eyes focused, Young stretched forward towards the line near the orange pylon with no time left on the clock. A ref in a black-and-white-striped shirt threw both hands up as a section of the crowd screamed in hysteria. I held my breath, waiting for the announcers' reassurance.

"Touchdown!"

I screamed and jumped up and down with the orange-clad fans on television.

"Texas touchdown, Vince Young! He's done it again!" the announcer bellowed.

Skye lifted her head off the couch, groggy. "What happened?"

"Texas. Texas won. Vince Young won!" I said.

She smiled, head back down, eyes shutting slowly.

"Good. That's really good."

I stayed in front of the TV and watched Vince Young receive his MVP trophy. I watched the footage of that definitive ten-second touchdown replayed and analyzed. I cheered every time they showed it.

The record was important, even if my father didn't think so. It was important that his record remain intact, on its own and without equal, given what happened to him as his time in college came to a conclusion.

Matt Leinart's career proceeded under the spotlight of celebrity fame and stardom after the Rose Bowl. It was predicted he would get picked up early in the NFL draft. After all, with just two college football losses, his record was impressive. But in 1972, despite my father's victories and undefeated performances, despite the fact that he had never lost a football game in high school or in college, my father's NFL future was far less certain.

The NFL draft was coming up, so I asked Dad what he thought of Ealey's chances. I knew he was small by NFL standards at five-eleven, although other quarterbacks his size had made it in the league. Dad shook his head. "Honey, Chuck Ealey probably won't get to play in the NFL," my father told me. "The NFL rarely lets black men play quarterback."

"But why not?"

"I wish I could tell you."[8]

What Christine Brennan's father did not know, however, was that my father would play a critical role in the outcome of the 1972 draft in a way that no one would have expected—a draft that would be historically significant for the National Football League and for our family, for two very different reasons.

21

I GREW UP believing that in the late sixties and early seventies there were no black quarterbacks in the National Football League. It turns out that cases of black quarterbacks in the NFL weren't unheard of at that time. They were just rare and complicated. It was a critical component of one of the most significant parts of my father's story, a part that was often misunderstood by those who knew the history. In search of clarification, I stumbled upon the stories of two key quarterbacks—Marlin Briscoe and Joe Gillingham.

Marlin Briscoe started to play quarterback at his predominantly white Omaha high school in the early sixties. He set league and college records in the position at the University of Nebraska. In 1968—the year of Dr. King's assassination and the year my father started at the University of Toledo—the Denver Broncos selected the Nebraska star in the NFL draft not for their quarterback roster, but to play a defensive position. During contract negotiations, Briscoe requested a three-day trial at quarterback, a request the Broncos coaching staff reluctantly said yes to. At the end of spring training, however, Briscoe was a dismal eighth on the quarterback roster, still slated for defensive back.

In a game against the Boston Patriots in September 1968, the Denver Broncos' starting quarterback broke his collarbone, and the backup struggled. Head Coach Lou Saban called on Marlin Briscoe. Briscoe completed his first pass and drove the ball 80 yards downfield for his first professional league touchdown. The Broncos went on to win 20–17.

On October 6, 1968, around the same time my father started to play at the University of Toledo with Don Fair and the Rockets, Briscoe walked onto the field to face the Cincinnati Bengals as the Denver Broncos starting quarterback—the first black man to start in the National Football League in that position.

"[Saban] didn't want to do it," Briscoe would one day say in an interview. "But they didn't have anybody else."

Briscoe started in seven other games with the Broncos that season, scoring fourteen touchdowns—a team record for a rookie quarterback that stands to this day. The following summer, however, the Denver Broncos held pre-season quarterback meetings without Marlin Briscoe.

Angered over the exclusion, Briscoe asked to be released from his contract and signed with the Buffalo Bills, where Jack Kemp was well established in the front-man position. Marlin "The Magician" Briscoe played out the rest of his career as an NFL wide receiver, eventually playing for the Miami Dolphins where the team won a Super Bowl during an incredible seventeen-game winning streak.

Briscoe retired from the league in 1976 and moved to Los Angeles. In race-torn L.A., Briscoe's life deteriorated dramatically. He became addicted to cocaine and lost his house and his championship rings when he defaulted on a bank loan. He was jailed twice and suffered a gunshot wound. Local dealers in his L.A. neighbourhood referred to him as "17-and-0" in memory of his glory days in football.

In my father's senior year of college, an agent from Dayton, who'd helped athletes from Ohio State University, approached him.

With the NFL draft quickly approaching, my father agreed to let the agent handle things while he finished up his courses.

"Just to be clear," my father told his agent. "I don't want to go as a defensive back. I'm not a defensive back. I'm not a wide receiver."

Aware of the stance most coaches took with regard to black quarterbacks, and aware of Marlin Briscoe's story, the agent informed my father that if he maintained his stance there was a good chance he wouldn't get drafted by anyone.

"I don't want to go to the NFL just to go to the NFL. I want to go as a quarterback," my father told him. "I've got my scholarship, my grades, and my education. If I can't play, I'll go to work."

The agent advised my father to write a letter stating his desire to only play quarterback, and his refusal to consider alternative positions. Prior to the draft, the letter was sent to all twenty-six teams in the National Football League.

Unaware of the letter that had been sent across the country, fans in Toledo anxiously awaited news about my father's NFL prospects. My father's agent started to negotiate with the professional football league in Canada.

When the results of the draft were announced, fans in Toledo, Portsmouth, and throughout the Mid-American Conference were disappointed with the outcome.

In seventeen rounds of the 1972 draft, no one picked Ealey. He had been eighth in the balloting for the Heisman Trophy in 1971. But in the draft, twenty-six NFL teams continually passed on him. Four hundred forty-two players were selected by NFL teams, but not Chuck Ealey.[9]

In the same 1972 draft, however, a black quarterback named Joe Gilliam was selected in the eleventh round by the Pittsburgh

Steelers. He was the first black man drafted as a quarterback by the National Football League, the same year my father was rejected.

Joe Gilliam would back up Terry Bradshaw in his rookie season. He would cross the picket line during a football strike in order to get his chance to start for the Steelers. He would maintain his starting position, albeit briefly, when Bradshaw and the others returned. But in 1975, a battle with cocaine and heroin would push Joe Gilliam towards retirement. He would go on to pawn both of his championship rings to feed an addiction that would ruin him.

Twenty-six NFL teams rejected my father in 1972 not because he was black but because of the only thing that set him apart from Joe Gilliam back then. They rejected him because of his letter. The way my father asserted himself was reprehensible to the white men running professional football teams across the country.

I told my father about my husband's and my encounter with the woman in the hotel convenience store in St. Louis when we got back to Canada, but he didn't say much about it at the time. A while later, however, my father wanted to talk about my response to her question: How did you get out?

I didn't have to get out. I was born in Canada.

"It wasn't going to Canada that got me out," my father said. "It was my education. Once I had that, that's all I needed. That was the difference."

My brother was in the room and so was Skye, my mother, and Mark. No one said anything. It's hard to tell someone like my father—someone who has done the things he's done—that he's wrong about his life-changing moment.

While I agree that a college education was important to my father's life, my father was wrong about what made the difference. Canada was critical. Marlin Briscoe and Joe Gilliam proved it. What happened in the NFL draft as a result of the letter was why my father left America. In so many ways, "getting out" hinged on my father's move to Canada.

CANADA
1972–Present

These shores of refuge, like the eternal shore,
often unite again, in glad communion, hearts that
for long years have mourned each other as lost.

HARRIET BEECHER STOWE,
Uncle Tom's Cabin

22

THERE WAS AN "I am Canadian" beer commercial that came out when I was in high school, where a fictitious man named Joe revealed all of the things that made him proudly Canadian. I remember waiting for the commercial to come on between TV shows so I could recite it. We were the second-largest land mass; we were the first nation of hockey; the beaver was a proud and noble creature. I also remember wondering what it meant if I didn't understand the comments Joe made about the toque or the couch, or what it meant if I didn't like hockey. I remember wondering if I could still be Canadian if I didn't look anything like Joe did.

What I realize now is that the similarities and differences between Joe and me were not important. The most important thing my father did for me was to make that epic statement true and accurate, regardless of what Joe and I had in common: I am Canadian.

That three-word sentence connected me to a different history. It explained the unique difference between my father and me, as a result of the place where my father was raised and the place he chose to raise me.

Because of the cold, Canadian winters, housing large numbers of slaves was impractical for the European settlers that started colonies in Canada. Wealthy colonizers who could afford extra help lived in large urban areas, not expansive plantation properties; they typically owned just one or two slaves, at most a handful—far different from the large numbers found on the cotton fields of America, where the growing season and the labour-intensive work of managing a rural property were continuous.

In the late 1700s, however, Britain abolished the slave trade entirely, enacting a law that was implemented in Canada soon after. But Americans in southern states continued to rely heavily on slave labour.

In 1850, the United States government passed the Fugitive Slave Act, which permitted the capture of any black person who could not produce proof of freedom. Free blacks and fugitive slaves in the north feared for their safety. Many travelled north into Canada, where freedom was available to those who succeeded in the dangerous journey.

American emigrant slaves travelled to Canada by foot, by boat, and by covered carriage. Some came on trains where they hid in the cars and compartments—helped by "conductors" like Harriet Tubman. Black men, women, and children departed from cities like Toledo, Chicago, Detroit, and Cleveland and settled in southern Ontario cities like Windsor, Toronto, Niagara Falls, and Hamilton—similar to the route my great-grandmother took when she left her family in Bristol, Tennessee, and moved to West Virginia, then to Portsmouth.

My father finished the final leg of the journey the first time he had travelled outside of America, when he arrived in Hamilton, Ontario, to meet with executives from the local professional football team.

"I remember coming up the hill, going to Hamilton," my father said of his visit in the spring of 1972. "I thought maybe it would be foreign. Something that was different. You think you're going to a foreign country," my father said. "Especially when you're in the U.S. You don't get any historical perspective about places."

I asked him what he thought of Canadians.

"I didn't get a real good read of the people until after I was there for a while," my father said. "I thought they were friendly. I didn't see a huge diversity issue. I didn't see a lot of black people either. Didn't see any foreigners—not a black area or anything like that."

"You didn't see any black people?"

"I saw a few on the street. But it wasn't like where you would go into a certain neighbourhood in a U.S. city and you would see more black people. You just didn't see that. It was just sort of dispersed."

I thought about the massive numbers of slaves who had lived in close quarters, and the crowded, segregated neighbourhoods where many black Americans still lived in destitute circumstances. I compared it to what I had seen in my Mississauga high school and at university, and what I now know about African Canadian history. Dispersed was a good word for Canada's black population—people who had come from different places, at different times, with different histories, spread out and in smaller numbers. It was why I felt so disconnected from other black Canadians.

It was difficult to make connections, to bridge the gap that divided us from one another.

When discussions about slavery and emancipation were reaching a critical point in the 1800s, the United States government established the Freedmen's Inquiry Commission, which was charged with investigating the condition of black American refugees who had settled in Canada a century before my father would.

It explained why my father's first impressions of Hamilton led him to the same conclusion I came to whenever I visited America as an adult, the same conclusion black American emigrants came to over a century earlier. Canada looked geographically similar to America, but it felt significantly different.

> For several years, the existence of freedom in Canada did not affect slavery in the United States. . . .; but [the number of black refugees] increased, early in this century; and the rumor gradually spread among the slaves of the Southern States, that there was, far away under the north star, a land where the flag of the Union did not float; where the law declared all men free and equal; where the people respected the law, and the government, if need be, enforced it.[10]

The refugees who were interviewed back then informed the commission that prejudice in Canada was rampant, that it was often worse than it was in America, but they also explained to the commission why they decided to stay and raise their families there, despite the prejudice. The *laws* in Canada supported freedom. Canada felt different to them because they were able to be truthful about their conditions and their hardships without fearing repercussions.

> In the South, they have motives for lying which do not affect them in Canada; for in the latter, it is evident that they have the most entire reliance upon the protection which the law gives them. Complain as they may about other matters, they all admit that; and it is a common

remark with them, that they are not now afraid to say things that are true, for "the law will bear them out in it."[11]

It pointed to what my father had been up against all of his life—a nation where the laws reinforced racism, segregation, and inequality. American laws created obstacles for basic rights and necessities—the right to date who you want; the right to live where you want; the right to pursue any job opportunity; the right to speak out against those who made pursuing those rights difficult.

My father grew up in a neighbourhood with few options and limited resources. The majority of men who looked like him were trapped in a system of inequality that had evolved from centuries of injustice. It included those who had served overseas, those who had never left their small towns, and those who had made it in professional football.

My father's first CFL contract was the opportunity my father had been working towards since he picked up those stones by the railroad tracks. It was a way to secure a different kind of life for his family doing exactly what he wanted. A way to be a different kind of man than the men he had known, a different kind of father—assertive and focused, instead of lost in hopelessness. That letter, those twenty-six rejections, and the contract that forced my father north saved our family.

23

PEOPLE called my family the Cosbys when I was growing up, even though the family's name on the show they were alluding to was the Huxtables. Even though Mr. and Mrs. Huxtable both had six-figure-income jobs and lived in a massive New York brownstone. My parents were nothing like them. My father was a financial advisor and my mother was a homemaker. I lived in a normal, suburban, Canadian household.

"I'm not rich," I told people. "My parents made me deliver newspapers in a wheelbarrow!"

But my father had played professional football. People thought he made so much money that he worked just for fun.

Other than indulging in brand new Lexus vehicles, my father has always been very conservative with his spending and private about his finances. I remember asking him how much he made when I was younger.

"Why?" he asked.

"I need to know for an application form."

"You need to know how much I make?"

"I need to know which range our household income is in."

"What's the last category?"

When I told him what it was, the one at the end with the most digits and the plus sign that signified an infinite range of money, he would say with his eyes fixed on whatever he was looking at, "Check that one."

I would smile, eyes wide and gaping as I checked the last box proudly.

"Are we rich, Dad?" I would ask him.

"*You're* not rich. Your mother and I might be rich, but *you* are not rich."

"I'll tell you something I've never told anybody," my father said, when we were sitting in his family room. "My first contract was $15,000 and three hundred dollars more if I started the game. I got a signing bonus of $5000 dollars. My second year, it was $30,000 and all the bonus stuff was taken out."

"Was that considered good?"

"One of the guys who was a second rounder for Oakland was about the same—$15,000 for the Oakland Raiders in 1972."

"How did that feel?"

"It was exciting, because that was more money than I had ever had. Period," he said.

It was not as much as NFL quarterbacks made at the time, but I don't think my father cared about that. He spoke of the agent who had arranged the letter to the NFL teams, who handled the contract with the CFL, and managed his finances during my father's transition to professional athletics.

"What was his name?" I asked him.

My father stopped, shook his head, then went on talking—a sign which always meant something.

"Was he a bad guy?" I said, interrupting.

My father considered the question, weighed his words carefully. "Well no, he wasn't a bad guy," he said slowly.

I leaned in, searched his eyes. "What?"

"I don't really want to say because I'm not sure."

"Daaad," I said.

"I think. I *think*," he said, squinting as though looking at something far away. "I don't know this but I think he had me sign a contract and they gave him some money just to get me to agree to sign. He got a kickback. I don't know that for sure, but before my second year, when I finally said, 'I can do this on my own,' he said I owed him some money."

"You owed *him* money?"

"They said, 'Well this is for what you may not pay us for.' So I said okay, I can't do a whole lot about it."

I shook my head, uncertain of how to proceed for a moment. "And then what?"

"I started negotiating contracts on my own."

My father backed up veteran Wally Gabler when he joined the Hamilton Tiger-Cats at the start of the 1972 season. Two games into the season, Gabler was struggling to lead the offence. In the third game, Coach Jerry Williams, a former coach for the NFL's Philadelphia Eagles, decided to make a change to the starting lineup.

On August 11, 1972, a crowd gathered to watch the much-anticipated quarterback from Ohio—a quarterback who had never lost a game of football. But in his inaugural appearance as a CFL quarterback, my father lost his first football game when in the final moments of the game a pass to the team's star receiver—who was wide open in the end zone—struck the goalpost.*

"Everyone always asks me what it was like to lose," my father told me, with a scowl on his face. He never liked that question. "I

---

* In Canadian football, the uprights stand on the goal line, in front of the end zone. The uprights stand at the back of the end zone in American football.

knew what it felt like to lose. I had lost in basketball. I had lost in track. I didn't like it, but I knew what losing felt like."

In game four, the Tiger-Cats lost again when a field goal attempt hit the goalpost. The team was now 1-and-3, but Coach Williams kept my father at quarterback.

"When he first came up here he left the pocket too early, but it wasn't long before he was sitting in there and picking out the right receiver," Williams said in an interview—an assessment that proved prophetic.

After losing his first two CFL matchups, my father led the Tiger-Cats to ten straight victories, earning them a spot in the playoffs as the highest-ranked team in the league's Eastern Conference. In the semifinals, when they played the Ottawa Rough Riders, my father recovered from a 19–7 deficit and went on to secure a spot in the Grey Cup. My father was named the league's Rookie of the Year as the 1972 season approached its conclusion.

A crowd of 33,000 fans sat in Hamilton's Ivor Wynne Stadium on December 3, waiting to see if my father would bring a Grey Cup victory to the home team Tiger-Cats.

American sportswriter Joe Marshall was in attendance, writing an article for *Sports Illustrated* about the politics of the NFL draft—about the undefeated black quarterback who was picked up by the Canadian Football League after the NFL rejected him, who was now playing in the CFL's Super Bowl equivalent.

On that windy, December day in 1972, the Ti-Cats added to their early lead against the Saskatchewan Roughriders when my father threw the ball 52 yards for a touchdown, making the score 10–0. The Roughriders, were led by the eleven-year veteran quarterback Ron Lancaster, however, who evened the score by halftime.

With two minutes left in the fourth quarter, the game was still tied. The Tiger-Cats were ninety-five yards from the end zone. With only three downs in Canadian football on a field that is ten yards longer than NCAA football fields, and with no timeouts available to them, Ti-Cat fans at Ivor Wynne Stadium braced themselves for a chilly overtime.

"Then Ealey started to work his winning magic," Joe Marshall wrote in his article.

My father threw three times in a row to tight end Tony Gabriel. With less than 40 seconds in the game, he threw to receiver Garney Henley, who made a sliding catch at the Roughriders' 26-yard line. One play later, clock ticking to zero, field goal kicker Ian Sunter booted the ball through the uprights to finish the game with a 13–10 victory for Hamilton.

My father earned additional notoriety, and a car, as the game's Most Valuable Player.

In his article for *Sports Illustrated*, Joe Marshall reflected on the game, my father's arm, his careful and impeccable aim and timing. He argued that, given his obvious talents and winning records, something unrelated to football must have influenced the NFL's decision to reject my father. He poked gaping holes in the NFL's explanation that my father's stature and the CFL's interest in him had affected their decision to pass on the undefeated Ohio native. Marshall asked my father how he felt about having to come to Canada to play quarterback professionally.

Sports Illustrated
December 11, 1972

CHUCK EALEY: CHAMPION AND STILL WINNER
Joe Marshall

[. . .] Ealey stood by his locker, dripping in champagne, Earl Grey's trophy on the bench next to him. To go with his rookie-of-the-year award, he had also earned a new car as the Grey Cup's most valuable player. And he could not keep a slight smile from flickering across his face. "I wonder what the NFL is thinking now?" the winner asked.[12]

"Winning the Grey Cup and becoming Rookie of the Year and MVP in the Grey Cup was really the high point for me," my father told me, nearly forty years later. "Every level that I wanted to get to and accomplish had happened. I realized in that moment that I could do this. I could do it on any level."

On December 23, 1972, three weeks after the Grey Cup win, my mother and father got married at a church back in Toledo—my father in black crushed velvet, my mother in creamy white lace with an olive-green ribbon around her waist. The stage was adorned with red Christmas poinsettias. They rented a place near Columbus before moving to Canada together in time for the 1973 Tiger-Cats' season.

At the start of my father's third season with the Tiger-Cats, the Eastern Conference moved from a fourteen- to a sixteen-game schedule. Each team was left to negotiate the change with their players—many of whom had already signed contracts that assumed a fourteen-game season.

"The guys wanted to get paid for the two extra games but [the Tiger-Cats organization] technically didn't have to pay them. Except for me," my father told me. "Because in my contract it said that they would pay me for fourteen games, and that I would get a bonus for every game that I started. They agreed to pay me for the two extra games, but the rest of the team didn't have that."

My father was concerned about how the decision affected his fellow teammates. So he and a few players—including key tight end Tony Gabriel—went to the local media. An article was published in the *Hamilton Spectator* that reflected poorly on the executives and the Tiger-Cats' general manager. The Tiger-Cats' organization responded by releasing and trading all of the players involved in the leak to the media midseason.

"Tony went to Ottawa, and I went to Winnipeg. Some other people got cut."

The trade to Winnipeg was filled with complications. My father would have to move further away from his mother, who was still living in Dayton, Ohio. He would spend the rest of the season out west while my mother stayed back in Hamilton at a time when the two of them were trying, with some difficulty, to start a family.

24

I WAS TAUGHT when I was younger to believe in a God who created the world in the beginning from His breath. I came to understand sometime during adolescence that that belief was not universally held. In fact, it seemed crazy to some people. Only when I looked at my father's story, it was so much harder to accept that things happen at random—that they weren't part of a bigger story.

In 1973, doctors discovered that my mother had a medical condition that would make it difficult—perhaps impossible—to get pregnant. She had been trying for a year, so the doctors gave her medication to help regulate her cycles. When it didn't work, my mother was devastated. As an only child, she had always dreamed of having a large family.

My mother had gone to church with her parents as a young girl, but she and my father had never talked about faith or religion. She had not thought much about God since her childhood. Until she needed a miracle. My mother opened a Bible she found in the house and started reading it in secret, as my father headed to Winnipeg.

Thirty years later, when Mark and I were trying to grow our own family unsuccessfully, I did the same thing. I prayed desperately over the thin pages of the very same book my mother had prayed over thirty years earlier: *Please, God, please. Give me a baby.*

What I didn't realize was how this act of faith and supplication connected me not just to my mother, but to my father and our family history. It was the final factor that would unite all of the things that had once felt muddy and uncertain.

Throughout the history of the slave trade, white slave owners used the Bible to perpetuate slavery. They promoted the apostle Paul's letters about the submission of slaves to their masters and requirements for dutiful obedience despite the host of ills slave owners justified with using misplaced scriptures. In exposing slaves to the Bible and the doctrines of Christianity, however, southern masters provided slaves with a resource that would shape a culture of resilience.

In the Bible, slaves would discover the story of the Israelites—a race of people who suffered great ills before their miraculous rescue, a story that conveyed a message of profound hope in the midst of destitute circumstances. In the Exodus story, American slaves would discover a God who was aware of suffering and who promised to help those who trusted Him wholeheartedly.

Slaves who embraced this Bible story believed that they would be delivered from their trials. They dreamed of freedom—their own promised land of Canaan where they would reunite with their scattered, broken family.

My mother turned to the book she was introduced to as a child on those wooden pew benches and prayed to a God she wasn't sure was there, about her desire to have children. She put her faith in a God whom the Bible said could do the impossible.

Later in the season, my mother discovered she was pregnant. So she kept on reading the Bible as my father, unbeknownst to her, started to do the same in Winnipeg.

"All the teams in the CFL were having Bible Chapel except for Hamilton," my father told me. "Your mother hadn't come out to Winnipeg yet and some of the players invited me to Bible Study. I said okay, but the big thing happened later."

At the end of the season, a few of the players from the weekly Bible Study my father was going to invited him to a conference put on by a group known as Athletes in Action.

Athletes in Action Letter — 1974

WHO AND WHAT IS ATHLETES IN ACTION?
Gordon Barwell

We congregate in arenas, stadiums and coliseums by the millions weekly to cheer them to victory . . . by the tens of millions we watch them on television.

The morale and prestige of cities—sometimes the entire nation—can rise and fall with their success or failure. Their professional and private lives are chronicled in newspapers, magazines, and on radio and television around the world.

Madison Avenue loves them, because through their high visibility and influence they can sell us products ranging from razors to racey cars. When they speak, we listen. What they wear, we wear. What they drink, we drink. What they do, we do.

They are athletes.
GOD-LIKE, BUT NOT GODS.

There is a mystique about them that has captivated every society and culture since Ancient Greece elevated the mythological Mercury and Hercules—as well as its real-life athletes—to near god-like status. More than winning in competition, athletes win honour, glory, prestige—and for some fortunes.

Yet they are not gods, they are humans. They have the same physical, mental and spiritual needs as non-athletes. They are not immune to human frailty [...]

At the four-day conference, athletes from professional Canadian sports teams exchanged similar stories about how faith helped them overcome hardships, helped them define something that had been intangible; it gave purpose and meaning to their lives when events seemed difficult, inexplicable, or meaningless.

"There was a guy by the name of Doc Ashalman," my father said. "I explained to him that I grew up in a Pentecostal Church, a Baptist Church, a Catholic Church, and all of those things, so I was quite knowledgeable about God and about Christ. And he said, you know, just because you walk into a garage it doesn't make you a car. Just because you walk into a church it doesn't make you a Christian. That's when I asked Jesus into my life. It's just a matter of your mind shifting from what you thought the do's and don'ts were, to understanding what grace is," my father told me. "To say, okay you're right, instead of just thinking that because you have all these things that you know about, it was just enough."

"So you always believed in God?" I said and he nodded as though that were obvious.

I realized it was. It was obvious in the way he stayed focused in the projects, despite his father—the way he cared for his mother and Bryant. It was obvious to anyone who had ever seen him play football that there was something inexplicable in him. Only something at the conference changed not only what he knew, but also how he thought and wanted to live.

"I think it's the upbringing that my mother and family instilled in me, and their professing that there was a God," my father said. "Young as I was, I believed. Because you grew up having to, in difficult times, really trust in what your parents showed you and believe in God. Whether you chose to follow God or not, you knew He was there. I think a 'head knowledge' turned into a 'heartfelt knowledge.'"

It was the first time I really understood how my father coped with unfortunate encounters, how he was able to move on and avoid the pitfalls of those around him. He did what people had done for generations before him—not the ones who simply acknowledged God's existence, but the ones who triumphed mentally and spiritually also. He put his faith in something bigger than his obstacles. He saw difficulties not as legitimate occasions for discouragement, but rather as occasions that required faith in a higher power, who was capable of unimaginable miracles.

When my father returned to Hamilton, that January 1975, he didn't talk about what happened at the Athletes in Action conference with my mother. Nor did my mother share about her praying and Bible reading.

Damon Christopher was born prematurely on April 15, 1975. It wasn't until after his birth that they faced a predicament, that my mother and father finally discussed what had happened in the months leading up to Damon's arrival.

"We should take him to church to get him baptized, or christened, or something," my mother says, as Damon cries inconsolably.

There are baby clothes and blankets strewn on the couch. Dishes are piled next to the sink in stacks that only seem stable.

"Well? What should we do?" she says to her husband, who's sitting at the table with the local paper and a coffee.

"I don't know," my father says, face buried in the business section.

"Maybe you should ask someone on the team?" she says, but my father says nothing. "Chuck?"

"Mmmhmm?"

"Maybe you should ask someone on the team."

He flips the newspaper down. "About what?"

"About church for the baby."

"In Winnipeg?" His voice is laden with criticism.

My mother places the baby in my father's lap, and my father lets go of the newspaper to hold the boy who's crying in shrill distress mode. She pulls the phonebook out of the kitchen drawer and thumbs through the pages: Cheyne Presbyterian Church.

"We want to baptize our baby," my mother says to a pastor the next day, the baby in her arms, as they sit down in matching chairs across from a man they have never seen before in a quaint office.

"Are you believers?" the pastor says.

"I went to church," my mother says.

The baby is quiet and so is my father.

The pastor—a white, middle-aged man in a beige shirt and thick-rimmed glasses—clears his throat. "What I mean is, have either of you been born again?"

He looks at my mother, then my father, then back at my mother again. My mother tries to process the words. *Born again.*

"I have," my father says.

My mother turns towards her husband, almost stirring the baby.

"What does that mean to you?" the pastor says slowly, eyeing my mother, who's bouncing the baby up and down more noticeably.

"I believe that Jesus Christ is the Son of God. That He's my Saviour," my father says, eyes on the pastor.

"When?" my mother says. "When did this happen?"

"At the conference," he says, turning towards her.

"The conference?" she says, voice high and exasperated. "In Winnipeg?"

My father nods. Across the desk the pastor fiddles with some papers.

"In January?" she says.

My father nods again. Five months ago. *Five months and he said nothing.* She thinks of her own Bible reading, her secret journey through the gospels.

"We're an evangelical church," the pastor says.

My mother shakes her head and looks to my father, but he's looking at a brochure on a nearby table.

"What I mean is, we don't baptize babies. We *dedicate* children. It means we help parents raise their children, in the hopes that one day—"

"Well then, we'd like to have him dedicated," my mother says.

The pastor in the dark-rimmed glasses looks at my father, but finds the young man hard to decipher. "Are you involved with a church in Winnipeg, sir?"

"Yes," my father says.

The pastor waits for a moment. "Maybe you and your wife should speak to someone there."

My father nods and puts the brochure back down on the table, standing to exit.

"So, that's all?" my mother says.

"I'm sorry for the confusion."

My mother stands and exits with the baby as my father shakes the pastor's hand. On the way back to the townhouse on Quigley Road, the hum of the engine and the bumps on the road echo in the silence.

A few weeks after the meeting at the Presbyterian Church, my mother read a letter from that same pastor. It recorded a famous conversation between two friends about what it meant to be born again, and offered my mother advice about how to make what she knew about God a part of her everyday living should she desire to. When she arrived in Manitoba, she heard a woman share her own born-again story. My mother decided there that that's what she wanted—a personal connection to the God she had been reading about in her Bible.

A few months later, my father was traded to the Toronto Argonauts. The Winnipeg Blue Bombers had hired a young star named Dieter Brock at quarterback, who was initially my father's back-up. My father and mother and their newborn son moved back to Ontario, where they bought a house in the suburb of Mississauga.

My mother and father's time in Winnipeg was short, but significant. It influenced why they raised us to believe anything was possible, even when things didn't go as expected. In 2008, when I found out I was pregnant, I made plans to teach those same lessons of faith to my own small miracle.

25

WHEN I was in high school, my family attended a Toronto
Argonauts game and sat near the fifty-yard line, among
a crowd of blue-clad Argo fans who were frantic and
hysterical. During the game, the Argos struggled offensively. The
veteran quarterback scrambled around the field and got sacked;
he repeatedly threw out of bounds to avoid being tackled.

A few rows down from us, a man turned to my father and
yelled, beer in hand, "Hey Chuck, they should put you in!"

My father pretended not to notice, but people in the crowd
started to join in as the quarterback's difficulties continued.

"Put Chuck in! Put Chuck in!" they shouted, louder and
louder.

People who didn't know what was going on turned, some
joined in the shouting. Cameramen and announcers took notice
and homed in on my father, who shook his head and laughed dismissively. When his image appeared on the Jumbotron, he stood
and waved humbly.

As I watched the current Argo quarterback try to make the
first downs on the field in front of us, for the most part unsuccessfully, I remembered something my father said when he watched
players move towards the close of their career in professional

athletics: It's always difficult, he would say, knowing when to end things, when to say you're finished.

CFL Illustrated — 1977
December 11, 1972

EALEY NEVER PANICKED
Pat Hickey

The first three games of the 1977 pre-season schedule weren't the most enjoyable of Chuck Ealey's career in the Canadian Football League.

The veteran quarterback didn't impress anyone as he struggled through a number of lacklustre performances.

But Ealey never panicked.

[...] Ealey is off to a flying start after two league games and there's little reason to doubt that he's picking up where he left off after his brilliant rookie season. A Grey Cup may be too much for Argo fans to hope for this year, but Ealey is providing the Argos with their best quarterbacking since Joe Theismann left town five years ago.

My father would continue to impress and entertain Argo fans. He would have moments in Toronto that reflected the talent, magic, and dying-minutes-of-the-game thrills of his college years and his CFL rookie season. But he would never make it to another Grey Cup.

"What's that?" I asked him as a child, my tiny, index finger gliding across a raised line of slippery skin that snaked in a pinkish line across the brown of his shoulder blade.

"It's a scar, where I had surgery," he told me.

I thought it was how his career ended—a devastating shoulder injury that took him away from the game. I didn't know how his career really ended until we were sitting in his living room talking, when I was nearly thirty.

"I said I was going to play five to seven years. It was the end of my seventh year and I said, Okay, it's time," my father said.

When my father started with the Toronto Argonauts, my mother was pregnant for the second time. Following his seventh year in the Canadian Football League, when Skye was almost two, my father began to arrange for his retirement from football. He retired in the late seventies, a year before I was born.

"When you start thinking about retirement, it's time to retire," he said.

My father pointed the remote towards the TV and flicked through the channels until he found a football game.

"I was asked to come back and play, but I said no," he told me, eyes watching players rumble and crash against one another. "It felt good to walk away from the game instead of having it push me away."

They must have asked him to come back when the season was about to start; my mother was pregnant with me, due that December. I once heard my father say that he stopped playing in the CFL partly because he said he would and partly because his family was growing. It was the first time I realized that my father had stopped playing because he knew that I was coming.

There was an interview my father did for a documentary on his career that was taped the weekend we went to Portsmouth in the summer of 2008. I listened to it for the first time two years later, when my one-year-old son was sleeping in the room next to me. It had taken more than a year for us to conceive, but three weeks after I started a new career, it happened. I gave birth to a healthy baby boy the following winter.

I could hear his deep sleeping breaths as I pressed the play button.

"What is your greatest accomplishment?" a man asked my father.

"Getting my kids to have respect for other people," my father said. "I don't think there's any more important responsibility than protecting my kids."

There was a pause before my father continued.

"One thing that I learned, you take a negative and—I get emotional about this—"

I could hear him swallow, his voice dropping low as he choked back something.

"—You take a negative of what happened with me and my dad," he said, "and you turn it into a positive because you want this to be the best for your kids."

They asked him what being a father meant, what he had maybe been missing.

"It's the need, the protection, the survival. To make sure every step along the way, they can get back."

I thought about his journey, about the beginning, and the end, and about the time I had spent going back in history to understand things, about what I would do now that things were clearer. Now that I embraced my life as a black Canadian with a history that was deeply embedded in America. Now that I was a mother. I was part of a long, powerful, heartbreaking legacy. I needed to appreciate the distance my father had travelled to save us—despite his imperfections.

"I'm not the outgoing father," he said.

I could hear in his voice the small smile that showed when he told a particular truth about himself that he knew might be a fault.

"I'm disciplined. I'm direct. But I've always had their best interests at heart."

I nodded and played the recording again and again, until I heard my son crying. I went and picked him up, my face wet with tears as I held his face in the curve of my shoulder and rubbed his back gently.

I have this vague memory of my father and me standing by the lake at the cottage. It's cool in the shadow of the evergreens, but the sun is out, and down by the lake tiny water waves glisten in the morning.

My father's standing on tightly pressed dirt, among crushed pine cones and needles, the ground beneath me muddy and mushy. My father picks up a small stone and tosses it. It skips and hops—*zip, zip*—into the water.

I pick up a stone from a pile near my feet and I toss it just like he did. *Plunk.* It disappears into darkness. I squint up at my father as the glow from above drapes his silhouette in sunshine.

"How do you do that?" I ask him.

My father shrugs his shoulders and laughs. He bends down, picks up another stone, and throws it. I watch it *zip-zip-zip* against the water, circles rippling, spreading outwards.

I pick up another rock and concentrate. I try to imitate him again. But my stone plunges straight down into the water. It doesn't zip forward.

My father pats my shoulder and says, "It takes practice."

He makes his way up the flagstone steps that lead back towards the cottage as I watch the concentric circles from our stones disappear against the shore where I'm standing. I throw one more stone and watch the circles spread outwards before climbing up the stairs after him.

Notes

1. *The Blade*, October 16, 2005.
2. *The Blade*, Toledo, Ohio, October 5, 1969.
3. *The Best Seat in the House*, p. 35
4. *The Best Seat in the House*, p. 34
5. *The Best Seat in the House*, p. 37
6. *The Blade*, Toledo, Ohio, December 29, 1971.
7. *The Best Seat in the House*, pp. 38–39
8. *The Best Seat in the House*, p. 39
9. *The Best Seat in the House*, p. 39–40
10. *The Refugees on Slavery from Canada West*, p. 4.
11. *The Refugees on Slavery from Canada West*, p. 10
12. Joe Marshall, "Chuck Ealey: Champion and Still Winner," *Sports Illustrated*, December 11, 1972.

Acknowledgements

Growing up, I often heard the familiar words, it takes a village to raise a child. I think the same thing goes for a book—doubly so, perhaps, for a memoir, where one person plays the role of telling the village's story. It is with a grateful and humble heart that I thank the village that stood alongside me and "raised" *The Stone Thrower*.

To my father and mother: Thank you for allowing me to share your story. You have put your best into raising your children, and your best is inspirational.

To Mark and Edan, you are my heart—essential, constant, life-giving.

Thank you to Damon and Skye and to all of the family that God hand-picked for me—to celebrate the good times and to sustain me through the valleys. To my nephews, who are precious.

Thanks to Aga, Kirsten, Jocelyn and Megan and to everyone who helped shape the story with their insight. To Karen Connelly, Judith Thompson, and Suzanne Primeau who each unearthed something in me before even I knew it was there.

Thank you to my MFA classmates and my MFA mentors for sharing their wisdom and carving out the writer in me. To the Ontario Arts Council for their generous assistance, and to the

Fieldstone Review who first published a section of *The Stone Thrower*.

Thank you to my Humber and University of Guelph-Humber colleagues.

Thank you to Don Fair and Larry Hisle for generously sharing their memories. Thank you to Al Bass, Tony Danini, Mary Berry, Mike Winkler, and the rest of the classmates at Notre Dame who provided their insight. Thank you to former classmates, friends and former teammates who are the subject of my memories—for your willingness to be a part of the story.

Thanks to *The Blade*, *Sports Illustrated* and other useful sources whose research and work helped inform the content of this book. A special thanks to Christine Brennan, for allowing me to use her work in this endeavour, and for being such a keen Rockets football fan.

Thank you to Charles Officer, John, Justin and Mike for the beautiful way they added another dimension to *The Stone Thrower*. To 90th Parallel, TSN and all their partners for supporting them in their efforts. Thanks to the Canadian Football League for their continued role in my father's story.

To Patrick Crean and Janice Zawerbny for their instinct and foresight, for seeing that underneath my first draft there was a good story and potential in a keen, unheard of storyteller. To Janice for the work she put in on her own dime and time; thank you to managing editor Wendy Thomas, copyeditor Erika Krolman, and Gordon Robertson for taking care of the details.

To the team at Thomas Allen & Sons Ltd., thank you for all of the passion you show in sharing this story. You are a wonderful part of this endeavour.

In writing this book, I have made use of a number of sources on topics such as the civil rights movement and other aspects of American history, and on accounts of my father's football career that appeared in newspapers, books, and magazines. The following is a list of these valuable sources:

Abu-Lughod, J. L. (2007). *Race, Space, and Riots: In Chicago, New York, and Los Angeles.* Oxford University Press.

Bachelor, R. E. (2009, December 21). *Slavery in Canada: Slaves Sold in Lower Canada During the 18th Century.* Retrieved January 6, 2010, from http://canadianhistory.suite101.com/article.cfm/slavery_in_canada.

Branch, T. (1998). *Pillar of Fire.* New York: Simon & Schuster.

Brennan, C. (2006). *Best Seat in the House: A Father, a Daughter, a Journey Through Sports.* New York: Scribner.

Brown, S. (1971). Negro Folk Expression: Spirituals, Seculars, Ballads and Work Songs. In A. Meier & E. Rudwick (Eds.), *The Making of Black America: Essays in Negro Life and History* (Vol. II). TN: Kingsport Press.

Cade, L. (1970). MU Put In Orbit, 52–53. *Huntington Herald-Advertiser.*

Columbia University. (n.d.). *Mapping the African American Past.* Retrieved June 17, 2010, from http://maap.columbia.edu/place/51.html.

Dickins, J. (1996). Memorable Labour Day Clashes. *Hamilton Spectator*, B3.

Greensboro Historical Museum. (n.d.). Retrieved 04 2009, from www. greensborohistory.org.

Hackenberg, D. (2005, October 16). *In their words: Coach left his mark on UT Football*. Retrieved July 2009, from toledoBlade.com: www. toledoblade.com.

Howe, S. (1865). *The Refugees on Slavery from Canada West*. Boston: Wright and Potter Printers.

Jares, J. (1971). Holy Toledo! Chuck Ealey Nearly Lost One. *Sports Illustrated*.

Joseph, P. E. (2006). *The Black Power Movement*. Routledge.

Marshall, J. (1972). Chuck Ealey: Champion and Still Winner. *Sports Illustrated*.

Moynihan, Daniel Patrick. (1965, March). *The Negro Family: The Case for National Action*. Retrieved May 6, 2009, from the U.S. Department of Labor: www.dol.gov.

Nixon, R. M. (1969, January 20). *Nixon's Inaugural Address*. Washington, D.C.

Pearson, H. (1996). *The Shadow of the Panther*. Perseus Publishing.

President's Commission on Campus Unrest. (1970). *The Report of the President's Commission on Campus Unrest*. Washington: U.S. Government Printing.

Rockets Rock Marshall. (1971, November 14). *The Blade*.

Sahadi, L. (2003, November 19). *Marshall football: From tragedy to triumph*. Retrieved January 7, 2010, from ESPN.com: http://a.espncdn.com/ classic/s/Classic_Marshall.html.

Shadd, A., Cooper, A., & Smardz Frost, K. (2002). *The Underground Railroad: Next Stop, Toronto*. Toronto: Dundurn Press.

Spofford, T. (1988). *Lynch Street: The May 1970 Slayings at Jackson State College*. Kent, OH: Kent State University Press.

Taylor, J. (1969, October 12). Ealey Keeps His Cool in Last-Second Win. *The Blade*.

Taylor, J. (1969, September 21). Rockets Fly High In Opener, 45–18. *The Blade*.

Taylor, J. (1969, October 5). Rockets in Orbit, Belt Bobcats, 34–9. *The Blade*.

Taylor, J. (1969, December 27). Rockets Rip Davidson, 56–33. *The Blade*.

Taylor, J. (1970, November 15). Snow, Mud, Dayton Can't Stop Rockets. *The Blade*.

Taylor, J. (1969, November 2). Toledo Bumps Miami. *The Blade*.

Taylor, J. (1959, November 23). TU Blanks Xavier, Finishes Perfect. *The Blade*.

Taylor, J. (1970, November 22). TU Rips Colorado State, 24–14. *The Blade*.

Too good to be real. (1973, July 14). *Canadian Football League Illustrated: Hamilton Tiger-Cats, IV* (2).

Unknown. (2000). The win in the wind Crot's field goal in 1969 capped rivalry's best game. *The Blade*.

Unknown. (2001). Accomplishments by TU athletic teams rich with contributions by men, women. *The Blade*.

Williams, R. L., & Youssef, Z. I. (1975). Stereotypes of football players as a function of positions. *American Journal of Sports Medicine, 3*, 7–11.